CYCLE TOURING

S

CYCLE TOURING - TOURING CYCLES

Chris Lucas

Blue Moon Press

First Published in the United Kingdom in 2011
by Blue Moon Press

A CIP record for this book
is available from the British Library

ISBN 978-0-9559603-1-4

Printed in England by Printforce Ltd., Bury

FOR

Jak and Jessica

Contents

Acknowledgments

Resources

All products featured in this book were available at the time of writing. Please contact the manufacturers/suppliers for details of any updated models.

Every effort has been made to trace the copyright holders of resource photographs and the author apologises for any omissions.

Illustrations

All illustrations and photographs are by the author.

Contributors

Many thanks are due to 'wheelman extraordinaire', Martin Chadwick, for his invaluable help in reading the text.

1

Introduction - Why Go Touring?

HG Wells once said: "When I see a man on a bicycle, I no longer despair for the human race."

The very first blueprint for a man-powered machine driven by pedals and cranks has been attributed to Leonardo da Vinci and dates back to the 15th century. By early Victorian times, such a machine had actually been constructed. Enterprising Scottish blacksmith, Kirkpatrick Macmillan, furnished his steel-framed bicycle with solid rubber tyres and used connecting rods to push the wheels. It can now be seen in the Science Museum in London. Later, rotating pedals were placed directly on the front hub of the bicycle, creating the famous 'Penny-farthing' - a strange contraption with an extremely large front and much smaller rear wheel, and paradoxically known as the 'ordinary'. In the 1890's, the 'safety' bicycle sensibly reverted to wheels of equal size turned by a crank and chain. So popular had cycling become by then, that in 1898, during the Easter weekend alone, over 30,000 cyclists were transported by train from Waterloo Station to the holiday resorts of the south coast. Since that time, surprisingly little in the basic design has changed, although modern bikes now come in racing, touring, commuter, mountain, folding, hybrid, tandem and even recumbent varieties.

From the beginning, man's need to go 'further and faster' has produced some amazing performances in the world of cycling. Olympic gold medals were being won as early as 1896 in the first Games of the modern era held in Athens, with a French cyclist, Paul Masson, taking home three. The highest speed on a bicycle (admittedly using a Chevrolet powered windshield) was achieved in 1973 - a remarkable 140.5 mph over a set distance of 1.2 km on the Bonneville Salt Flats in Utah. As for endurance, Englishman Thomas Goodwin attained an incredible record in 1939 by covering over 75,000 miles in a year - an average of 205.65 miles per day. And following the usual pattern of losing out to the Germans, Goodwin's achievement was completely dwarfed by a certain Walter Stolle of the Sudetenland, who cycled 402,000 miles in an 18 year long tour that finally ended in 1976. Taking in 159 countries and sustaining more than 1000 punctures, he proudly claimed that he hadn't suffered a single day's illness during his little outing. After eventually hanging up his bike, Stolle emigrated to southern Spain, where he spent the rest of his life growing fruit trees.

In 1978, another biking eccentric, Bob McGuiness, completed the 3,976 mile crossing of Canada on a unicycle, setting a time of 79 days. Even further along the path of eccentricity is the recent feat of Londoner Joff Summerfield who circumnavigated the world on his hand-made Penny-farthing. Pedalling east and wearing a pith helmet, he returned two and a half years later, having once been mugged, twice hit by lorries and somehow managing to reach Everest base-camp at 17,000 feet, en route. What on earth could have possibly motivated these strange albeit extraordinary deeds? And where has our great love affair with the bicycle come from?

Cycling, in whatever form it takes, seems to hold a rather special place in our affections. Whether or not we choose to continue in later life, as children, nearly all of us have experienced those first wobbly steps in the brave attempt to balance on two wheels. How good it feels when we finally master this awkward skill. How natural it soon becomes to turn and lean and twist, and how quickly we realise that here is a vehicle that suddenly presents us with our first real opportunity of freedom. Gone are the shackles of overbearing parents; gone are the restrictions of getting from A to B on foot or having to travel by bus. The excitement of the 'bike ride' has arrived, bringing with it a passion for adventure and a yearning to be thrilled by the unknown. Journeys can be planned, maps pored over, new horizons explored and, at the end of the day, we're still left with an object that can be cleaned, polished, oiled, loved and tinkered with to our heart's content. Is it any wonder that, for many of us, the bicycle subconsciously represents all that was good about childhood?

So, our deep attachment to the bicycle can be thought of as being almost genetic. This is the machine that took us to school, to the shops, to our best friend's house and, when we were feeling a little more adventurous, out through the dusty suburbs and into the country - seminal events in our early development, which are never completely forgotten. These ingrained, distant memories lie dormant, quietly coursing through our veins until, one day, they rise like a phoenix from the ashes to reawaken and renew our long lost love of cycling. For those of us who eventually take up the gauntlet again, whether it's mountain biking along dried-up river beds or time-trialling at the velodrome or performing acrobatic tricks on a BMX circuit, there will always be a small part of our cycling DNA that is forever associated with childhood exploits of leaving home with a map and a sandwich, heading for a land far away. Maybe, it's just that we're the ones who crave adventure, who see two-wheeled deeds of daring-do as being as exciting as Christmas morning - who have never quite grown up. Yet, once you allow yourself to give in to it, touring by bike is every bit as obsessive and addictive as other forms of cycling and, despite the challenges, can be more stimulating, more enjoyable and far more rewarding.

Obviously, cycle touring will mean different things to different people. For some, it's a day-trip to the country, perhaps along a canal towpath or a cycle trail, soaking up the fresh air and the scenery. For others, the boundaries are expanded to circular routes involving days away and stopovers in B&B's or Youth Hostels. Whether riding alone or as a family or in a group, these longer tours inevitably require a greater degree of planning and practice. Having a reasonable level of fitness is fine for a one-off trip of 20 miles or so. To complete a week in the saddle, averaging distances of 40 or 50 miles, day after day, demands a little more. You'll need to get some honest preparation under your belt before you even think of setting off - easy rides at first, building up slowly towards your daily goal and, if possible, taking in some hill work for good measure. But soon enough, weekend excursions and more ambitious journeys will become the established norm rather than the painful exception. You're halfway there to becoming irretrievably hooked.

The ultimate 'cycle tour' experience - the expedition - can, in turn, be seen as merely an extension of this. There is nothing to fear, as they say, but fear itself. Coast to coast, Land's End to John O'Groats, trans-European tours, cycling across America or even pushing body and machine around the world, are journeys often taken on by fairly ordinary human beings. The key to their success is dogged determination, lots of organisation and hard work, and never, ever having to say 'What if ...?' or 'I only wish ...'

For each and every one of us, our sometimes mundane existences are occasionally punctuated by 'if only's'. Some are trivial, such as 'if only I'd put £10 on the winner of the Grand National ...' - while others become life-changing and may cause deep, nagging regrets. I'm not suggesting that we should all place ourselves in the enviable position of dropping everything and remortgaging the house, so that we can attempt the north face of K2 or spend a couple of years cycling Pole to Pole. Few of us have the time, let alone the means or the inclination in our otherwise busy and hectic lives, to selfishly do exactly what we want.

More often than not, though, regrets can be generated by hesitatingly saying 'no' to perfectly attainable ambitions and turning down anything that vaguely means taking a risk. Responsibilities, commitments, wives/husbands, children and grannies must, of course, come first in the bigger scheme of things, but if we're brutally honest with ourselves, these obligations are often used as a convenient excuse for doing nothing rather than something. The fear of tackling one of life's 'little adventures', the hardship created by the cost and effort involved and the embarrassment of possible failure or making mistakes - factors that children dismiss with barely a second thought - suddenly become insurmountable obstacles. Risk, by definition, is bound to include an element of having to overcome difficulties and a more than reasonable chance of making the odd silly mistake along the way. How we deal with these setbacks and slip-ups, however, is the true measure of our worth.

Even successful cycling exploits can produce uncharacteristic and, at times, simple errors of judgment. Like any other mortal, young Scotsman, Mark Beaumont made a few fundamental blunders in his recent 18,000 mile 'round the world' record-busting cycle tour. Engineering adjustments to the back wheel of his 'state of the art' bike, to incorporate hub-type gears, caused broken spokes and repeated punctures on the first leg of his trip across Europe. The inability to decipher the Cyrillic alphabet left him with problems in map reading and understanding road signs in the Ukraine and Bulgaria (learning the 'Russian' symbols would have taken him no more than a few hours). Then there was the crucial oversight of travelling through Pakistan and India during Ramadan, leaving him hungry and unable to find food during daylight hours. Why, also, did he rely on a summer-grade sleeping bag in the frozen wastes of North America in midwinter? Obviously, he got a lot more right than he got wrong, but all of this coming on the back of three long years of careful planning and preparation only goes to show that even the 'mother of all cycle tours' can, on occasion, be found wanting due to human error. It's comforting to think that when you're making your own stupid gaffes, you are at least in good company.

Encouragingly, many far less intrepid adventures than that of Mark Beaumont's are well within the scope of the average cyclist, both in terms of time and money. A good touring/hybrid bike can be had for as little as £500 and a two or three week trip needn't cost you any more than a cheap summer holiday. Expensive cycling equipment and clothing can be 'down-sized' and minimised. There's no real need to come dressed as 'Lycra Man' with skin tight, bulge revealing, multicoloured, DayGlo shorts, longs or even three-quarters. They might look great on the road, but lose all sense of dignity when walking round town or strolling down the aisle of your local supermarket. The world of Camelbak hydration bags, no-tears sunglasses, heart rate monitors, GPS receivers, fancy pumps, fancy lighting systems, £100 plus helmets and fancy cycling shoes can all be readily sacrificed in the cause of common sense and cost. Just like dads dancing badly at a wedding (at a certain age, it becomes politic to sit it out), those trendy Lycra cycling pants can easily be replaced by ordinary, padded shorts. A breathable, waterproof jacket is a more than satisfactory substitute for that expensive winter biking kit. Rather than buying 'top of the range' helmets, locks, gloves, lights, bike bags and everything else, perfectly functional alternatives can be obtained at perfectly affordable prices. And there's absolutely nothing wrong with an old-fashioned bike bottle for taking on water.

So, everything is 'doable' if the motivation to do it exists. For some, the motivation might be based on a drive to get fit. We all know that inactivity plays a major part in the onset of many illnesses and also promotes overweight and obesity. Recreational cycling, which can be tailored to include the whole family, is the ideal foil and can often prove to be the springboard to greater things. Here are a few random considerations:

- It's recommended that adults take 30 minutes moderate exercise 5 times a week - cycling 4 or 5 miles a day would satisfy this.
- Cycling on a regular basis gives you a level of fitness equivalent to someone 10 years younger.
- Cyclists are more likely to live longer than non-cyclists.
- On busy roads, contrary to popular belief, you are more exposed to pollutants when in a vehicle than on a bike.

- Coronary disease (including heart attack) is reduced by 50% if you're a regular cyclist.
- Cycling, like swimming, gives an excellent cardiovascular workout without putting too much stress on the joints (unlike football, running, kick-boxing and other forms of violence).
- As both an exercise and an escape, cycling can help to de-stress our frantic life-styles.
- Regular cycling leaves you mentally more active and alert further into old age, delaying dementia and similar variations of senile lunacy (I hope!).

Other incentives hinge on practicalities and economics. Touring on two wheels is the perfect pace for exploring both town and country - faster than on foot and allowing you to stay in contact with your surroundings in a way that's impossible by car. There's no need to carry a heavy rucksack when a set of bike bags can take the strain and no crippling parking or fuel costs to take into account. Urban cycle ways and a growing National Cycle Network now provide easy routes through Britain's towns and cities and, with a little judicious planning, busy open roads can be avoided altogether by switching to country lanes, canal paths, disused railway lines or bridleways.

There is also a healthy social side to touring by bike, whether alone or in a group. The solitary cyclist will always come across like-minded people along the way or at the overnight YHA stop, while travelling with a set of friends has its own obvious advantages from a social viewpoint. Then, there's the increasingly popular long distance charity ride, in which organisations will arrange trips to far-off exotic places in return for fund raising - a great way of meeting people and visiting new countries that would otherwise be out of financial reach.

Cycling in general and cycle touring in particular, caters for all ages and all needs. There are no fixed rules, no age or gender restrictions, no set distances to be completed and the pace of travel is up to you. Far more economical and less stressful than the car if travelling to work is your concern. Cheaper than annual gym membership fees if it's fitness you're after, and extremely family friendly and sociable for the day-tripper. And for those of us with 'itchy feet' and the desire to take the odd risk or two, the bicycle is an affordable and practical means of seeking adventure and living the dream.

Tempering that risk with common sense will obviously demand a certain measure of risk assessment. Even the weekend outing to the country requires some thought, if only to consider basic safety or to check out the route and the bike before setting off. The longer the trip, the greater the need for detailed preparation, but this doesn't have to be an onerous task - in fact, planning can add to the overall enjoyment. I've always found that half the fun is sitting by the fire on a cold winter's night with maps, books and lists, working out stopovers and distances, and researching what's on offer in the cities (or the countries) you hope to cycle through the next spring or summer.

In the chapters that follow, I've tried to take an objective view of the cycle tour and the touring cycle, but will freely admit to it being slightly coloured, even restricted, by my own experiences and fiscal circumstances (not necessarily a bad thing). Many cycling books supply such a mass of options and opinions on equipment, fitness, clothing, accessories, safety, maintenance, routes, etc., not forgetting the bike itself, that the reader is left a little bewildered and, in some cases, frightened off. Undoubtedly, information is power - but too much information can sometimes only serve to confuse. I have attempted to cover all of the above aspects and more, although I've limited any facts and advice to the subject in hand - i.e. touring by bike without it costing a fortune. I've also tried not to lose sight of the main aim, which is to convince the 'would be' distance-cyclist that he is capable of much more than he imagines as far as touring is concerned, and to show him what's available in the pursuit of that goal. I would like to think that if these pages manage to inspire just one cyclist to cancel the bargain summer package trip and, instead, head off happily into the sunset on his bike, then my efforts won't have been in vain.

2

Types of Cycle - The Modern Mix

Our first task is to briefly define, describe and, afterwards, dismiss the growing and, at times, mystifying list of different types of bike available. The touring cycle and the hybrid (which, in itself, has recently become an 'anything goes' and therefore confusing term) can then be looked at in greater detail.

Mountain Bike

Sometimes referred to as the ATB (All Terrain Bike), the mountain bike, like the 4th of July, Rap music and Spam, was born in America. As the name implies, its origins are to be found in competitive downhill racing on rough mountain trails in the shape of beat-up, modified road bikes. Gradually, it evolved into the popular machine we all know and love

- lightweight frame, suspension forks, straight handlebars and smaller 26 inch, wide-rimmed wheels with heavy, energy sapping tyres.

Stable and tough on the track and great for short-haul commuting, it can now be found in the role of the police bike, postie's bike, the courier bike and, because of its comfort and manoeuvrability, is also the automatic choice of the urban cyclist. Triple chainset front cogs and a rear cassette of anything up to 9 speeds, the derailleur gear has a range that's designed for acceleration, uphill climbing and maintaining balance in difficult terrain. Although perfectly adequate for touring purposes, the major drawback of the mountain bike remains the amount of customising needed (mudguards, racks, tyres, etc.) to make it a more viable proposition for long treks. In raw form, it is most definitely the domain of the weekend cyclist who enjoys the mud and the adrenalin rush of off-road biking.

Nowadays, mountain bikes fall into one of two main categories. The general purpose 'hard-tail' has a rigid frame with front suspension forks, while the 'full susser' enjoys the added comfort of rear suspension for rough riding on rocky trails and fast downhills. From cheap and nasty 'his and hers' versions to high-spec five grand machines with titanium or carbon frames, traction control and disc brakes, and boasting names such as 'Rockhopper' and 'Bigfoot', they span the complete spectrum of component cost and quality - in other words, you get very much what you pay for.

Racing Bike

The road racer, like the mountain bike, is difficult to modify for touring and has the added disadvantage of a distinct lack of low gears. Most come with a double chainset at the front of their derailleur system, combined with an 8, 9 or 10 speed rear cassette.

Even in the mid-market range, racers are expensive. At the upper end, they can cost as much as a small car and weigh as little as 13 lb. Armed with lightweight carbon-fibre frames, integrated brake and gear levers and narrow alloy wheels with ultra-slick tyres to cut down rolling resistance on the road, these are frisky machines that are built for pace. The tight frame geometry means a relative lack of comfort, with the rider aerodynamically arched over his bike in an attempt to cut down on wind resistance. Depending on the road surface, the ride can be bumpy and unforgiving - everything is focused on making A to B as fast as is humanly possible. Without doubt, strength has been sacrificed to the god of speed and the stick-thin tyres can be prone to punctures, although with recent British success at the Olympics, both road and circuit racing have become increasingly popular. This is cycle sport for the real enthusiast and fitness freak and, as well as competitive outdoor racing, a mind-boggling array of events now takes place indoors, including Team Pursuit, Madison, Keirin, Time-trial and Omnium (none of which I would really care to expand upon).

City Bike

A new breed, which can be traced back to the old 'town and country' bike of the past superimposed onto a modern mountain bike frame. They are often introduced in glossy brochures as 'urban cycling with attitude', 'city slickers with expression obsession' (whatever that means), or as the machine that 'cuts a swathe through the suburban jungle'. The market is aimed at everyone from those searching for a healthier lifestyle, to the 'tree-huggers' wanting to reduce their carbon footprint and save money while saving the world. These are the bikes that can be seen tethered outside trendy coffee-shops, or carrying small children in child seats on the school run, usually ridden by people wearing extremely expensive helmets.

Sideswipes aside, the city bike is undoubtedly an excellent mode of transport for the city. The same upright riding position as the mountain bike, with 'comfort' saddle, straight handlebars, weight bearing hubs and bike rack, it also comes with a lighting system, bike stand, full mudguards and a chain guard to protect clothing. The ladies' bike is usually 'step through' and both gender versions can be upgraded with 8 speed hub gears and ultra efficient disc brakes. Everything is aimed at low maintenance and middle-class street cred.

Folding Bike

Small, but perfectly formed (as they say), the modern folding bike was developed from the 'sixties' shopper - a revolution at the time, although now just another slice of cycling memorabilia.

The 'folder' ranges from £150 to well over £1000, and is variously designed with different types of frame, folding arrangement and wheel size (anything from 16 inch to 24 inch). These bikes have filled a definite niche in the market and are so popular with urban commuters that, for some, demand has outstripped supply. Compact and light enough to put in the boot of your car or take on a train or tram, names such as Brompton, Birdy and Dahon seem to appeal to the posher end, while larger manufacturers, like Giant, produce their own excellent versions. Easy to assemble and quite versatile for shorter road journeys, many models come with derailleur systems, while others have 4 to 8 speed hub gears. Accessories can include anything from integral rollers, which make the bike easy to push around when folded, to front suspension, handlebar compasses and immobilisers; most have mudguards and racks as standard. One novel departure, described as 'ready to use straight from the bag', is the Bike-in-a-Bag, the ultimate small-wheeler, which does 'exactly what it says on the can', making it even more convenient for the commuter and costing less than £250.

Although very much limited as far as length of journey is concerned, whichever make or model you choose, the design and quality of components reflect an increasingly strong and growing market; all the problems associated with small-wheeled bikes of the past have been largely eliminated.

Power Assisted Bike

Hardly a credible contender on the touring scene, but worth a mention all the same, having answered the prayers of cycling's 'hill haters'. With lightweight frames, and some looking remarkably similar to their urban

commuter cousins, they carry battery power-packs offering up to 80 miles range before needing a recharge. The electric motor is usually located on the front wheel hub and is activated by a switch or twist-grip mechanism, giving either assisted or total power drive when pedalling becomes too tiresome. Again, a variety of frame shapes, wheel sizes and gear systems are available, with one company nostalgically reviving the old 'shopper' in power form, complete with handlebar basket and 24 inch wheels. These bikes don't come cheap though - £700 to £1500!

Recumbent Bike

Another strange looking machine, where the cyclist sits in a seat rather than on a saddle as he pushes the pedals in an almost horizontal direction (hence 'recumbent'). Better than you'd imagine for long distance touring, they can sometimes be seen on the road towing yak trailers piled high with mountains of luggage. All the usual equipment and accessories are present (V-brakes, derailleur gears, lighting systems, etc.) and, because of their elongated rigid frame with rear suspension struts, they afford easy comfort to the rider. Like the electric power-assisted bike, recumbents are costly - you'd be lucky to get one for under £1200.

Others

There are, of course, other variations and 'oddities' in cycling hardware, although it has become increasingly difficult to accurately define all types. Shades of grey upon grey have now produced an extremely wide spectrum of machine capable of suiting every purpose and every pocket. Nebulous versions of the city bike include the street bike (basically a road bike with straight handlebars), and the urban/utility bike (a city bike minus all the bits, usually finished in trendy matt black with slick tyres and all black components). Different manufacturers seem to have their own particular slant on this end of the market and the choice of what you can get for your money is mind-blowing. Some veer more towards mountain bikes; others are virtually tourers with trekking or hybrid frames and 26 inch wheels. A further mutation is the single-speed bike and its fixed-wheel offspring, one notably made by Condor. Light and simple and easy to maintain, these are ever growing in popularity, especially in the bigger towns and cities where they are much favoured by the cycle courier.

Then, there's the tandem, which has been going for as long as anything else of consequence in biking history - often tailor made to order and therefore quite expensive. Reasonably priced 'off the shelf'

tandems are made by Dawes and sport wide-range Shimano gears, disc brakes and optional 26 inch or 700c wheels; one model has even downsized the rear frame to accommodate the junior rider.

Another throwback to a bygone era of style and Sturmey-Archer gearing is the retro (or 'heritage') bike. Classic looking, having rear rack, full chain guard, curved handlebars, dynamo lighting and sprung leather saddle, all the latest technology is cleverly incorporated, although not immediately apparent. An interesting blend of the modern and the traditional, it is seen, by some, as the very height of 'cool'.

Finally, and a far newer 'look' is the mini bike - more accurately, mini 20 inch wheels set in a rigid and slightly odd shaped frame with a choice of either flat or drop handlebars. Again, unashamedly aimed at the city commuter market and, in particular, at those who want to be seen on something different, it does manage to tick all the boxes of being light, compact and strong, and also rides well on busy roads.

Leaving this bewildering array behind, we can now go on to examine the modern touring bike and the classic hybrid (the hybrid of mountain bike frame and road bike wheels). Although these are two quite different machines (see pages 34 to 37), they both possess the same qualities of strength, reliability and comfort - so important when distance-cycling.

3

The Touring Cycle - Fit for Purpose

A biking workhorse - tough on the track and fast on the road. It's just a matter of getting your head round the fact that it can also lay claim to its fair share of street cred.

Advantages and Anatomy

Funnily enough, the best machine for cycle touring is the touring cycle, with the hybrid coming a close second. Cannondale, Dawes and Trek are just some of the major companies who sell a range of 'tourers', while hybrids (in one form or another) are produced by most bike makers. You can, of course, use anything you wish to eat up the miles - mountain bikes, road/racing bikes or even a 'folder', but all of these have distinct disadvantages. Mountain bikes run on thick, knobbly tyres producing too much road friction and have no frame fittings for pannier racks or mudguards. Racing cycles aren't sturdy enough to carry the load, don't possess particularly low gears and can be pricey, and folding bikes, while great for commuting, have limited long-distance potential due to gearing and sprocket size.

   Although everything can be transformed, adjusted and modified to do the job, a reasonably inexpensive touring bike already has the ideal frame geometry and strength for any length of journey, together with the best 'on board' equipment for you and your baggage. These are the bikes that possess the perfect credentials - whether it's travelling to work, riding down the towpath of the Shropshire Union Canal for the weekend, enjoying a family cycling holiday round the coastline of East Anglia, or taking on a route from northern Spain over the Pyrenees and up through France. They don't look out of place on tracks and bridleways; their gearing is such that inclines provide no problems and, even when loaded, they prove extremely pacey on long stretches of tarmac. When fitted with panniers (back and front), the touring bike is balanced and feels comfortable. It's tough enough to carry as much as you can pack into its bags and designed to give optimum support to body and limbs, so as to minimise aches and pains at the end of the day's cycle.

With the encouragement of market forces, like everything else, the touring bike has moved on. The traditional British made load lugger of yesteryear, with drop handlebars and heavy steel frame, has now been persuaded to cheerfully embrace all recent innovation and styling. Though still viewed by the uninitiated as being merely the predecessor of the first hybrids, these are, in fact, two very different 'animals' - but two bikes, which for touring purposes, have a lot in common. Lightweight alloy frames, flat or butterfly (figure of 8) trekking bars, strong 700c wheels, powerful V-brakes and wide-range Shimano gears are just some of the options to be found on both the modern tourer and the hybrid. In the end, it's a matter of personal choice.

Ergonomics and modern technology have also recognised the need for all breeds of bike to become more female-friendly, and the tourer and hybrid are no exceptions. Manufacturers have finally had to accept the glaringly obvious - that male and female bodies are different - and, within the industry, a lot of science and effort has been aimed at developing cycle design for women. Smaller upper body and, on average, greater thigh length has affected every aspect of the basic frame shape of the ladies' bike and a good deal of thought has also gone into its overall styling. Gone are the days when the only concession to the fairer sex was to build the 'step through' model, so that they didn't have to lift their skirts before setting off. Many bikes now use unisex frames, while others have slightly reduced top tubes to allow for a woman's shorter torso and reach, combined with taller head tubes to create a better riding position. Some have kept the traditional slanted top tube, but with the addition of specially shaped saddles and smaller diameter handlebars, comfort has been greatly improved. Cycling has had to bow to the fact that, no matter what aspect of the sport is involved, female participation is growing fast. All the brochures now devote entire sections to women's bikes, often setting out their 'female-specific' range on bright pink pages - how times have changed! As far as touring bikes are concerned, modern frames tend to be unisex with geometry and ancillary equipment able to accommodate both genders, while most hybrids come in distinct gents and ladies versions.

Regardless of gender or anything else, however, and despite all the technological advances of recent decades, there are still just five crucial points where your body touches your bike - two on the pedals, two on the handlebars and last, but not least, one on the saddle. Bearing this and other key factors in mind, the ways in which the tourer fulfils the objective of easy riding to greatest advantage, are as follows:

1. A lightweight frame geometry created for comfort and positive steering.

2. Drop style or modern trekking handlebars, allowing for a variety of hand positions.

3. Saddle (with optional suspension seatpost) anatomically designed for distance-cycling.

4. Toe-clip or demi-clip pedals, for better efficiency on hills.

5. Larger (700c), wider-rimmed wheels with 36 to 40 spokes, built for durability and to make the bike versatile enough for riding trails and tracks.

6. Rigid front forks with no suspension (front suspension only serves to drain your pedal power on roads and isn't designed to be laden with panniers).

7. Ideal gear ratios using a triple chainset front and 8/9 speed rear freewheel, and with a gear range suitable for steep uphills as well as giving optimum speed on the flat.

8. Mudguards and rear pannier rack as standard, together with fittings for front racks (giving better weight distribution).

9. 32mm/38mm semi-slick tyres for added comfort and improved road performance.

10. Smooth 'click-shift' indexed gear change and sharp V- brakes.

Most of these features also apply to the hybrid bike, and those that don't, can easily be modified to do so.

So, whether it's short journeys or long-haul trips you've got in mind, the touring cycle (and many hybrids) meets all the criteria demanded for reliability, comfort, strength and efficiency. Everything is aimed at making the rider as relaxed and comfortable as possible. Its frame, wheels, tyres, gears and brakes are specially designed to carry the load, both on the flat and when grinding up steep inclines and over hills. Its ancillary equipment - handlebars, saddle, racks and mudguards - are shaped to ease the impact on body and soul on even the longest of treks. And, perhaps most importantly, these design features enable the cyclist to continue resolutely along that tarmac trail, day after day after day.

The following gives a detailed anatomy of the touring bike and an equally thorough analysis of what works best and why, providing further insight into its suitability for ticking off the miles when distance-cycling becomes the main objective. This is a graphical and comprehensive description of all that makes these machines work well under load and over distance. It is a picture of why the touring bike is 'fit for purpose' and why, ultimately, it beats the competition.

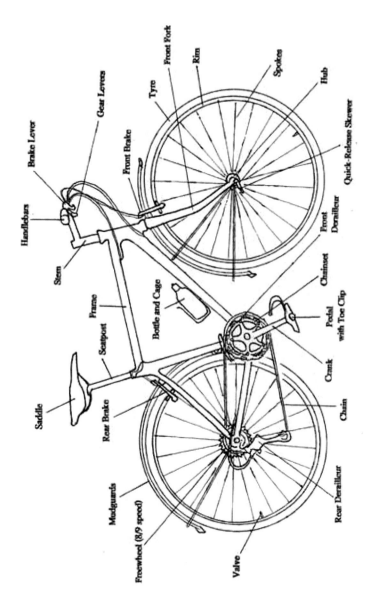

Anatomy of the Touring Cycle

Frame

The heart of any good bike is a good frame. Living in a world flooded with new technology, touring frame construction (as all other aspects of cycling) has inevitably become a function of computer aided design and scientific research. The holy grail of strength, lightness and rigidity has been relentlessly pursued in the name of maximizing performance without sacrificing comfort.

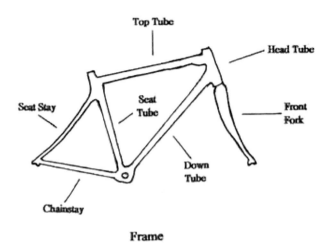

Frame

A tourer's geometry is more compact than others, with a shorter top tube and a more laid-back seat tube angle. This relaxed frame geometry makes for added comfort, an upright riding position and positive steering. The downwards slope of top tube towards the seat produces a shorter wheelbase, which lowers the frame's weight and increases 'lateral' stiffness, and because lateral stiffness reduces loss of energy by avoiding flex, the bike's performance is improved. In turn, to compensate for this rigidity, comfort is achieved by using a more forgiving material in the forks. Modern composite materials are now able to take a lot of the vibrations out of the road, with obvious benefits on longer rides.

So, a good combination would be an alloy frame that's compact and light, together with carbon composite or chromoly front forks. These need to be of the 'rigid' variety as, for touring purposes, the idea of front suspension forks is a definite 'no-no' - too much human energy is absorbed by suspension forks when pedalling on tarmac. There should also be enough clearance to accept mudguards, and front forks and rear seatstays should have eyelets/bosses for those all important pannier racks.

Although standard alloy frames are extremely light, if weight isn't such an issue, a steel frame can offer both strength and flexibility where it's needed. Not as daft as it seems, many long-distance cyclists swear by the virtues of steel frames, and good ones are reasonably light as well. The best are historically made by Reynolds. These frames use butted tubing that varies in thickness, giving strength where it's required, so reducing weight where it isn't. The Reynolds 531 (531 is the ratio of elements making up the manganese-molybdenum-steel) is, amongst others, an excellent lightweight steel option.

Tyres

The sizing of tyres is confusing. Imperial or metric, 26 inch or 700c, the choice of wheel and tyre is yours, though most touring bikes run on the larger (27.5 inch) 700c. Both sizes relate to the diameter of the tyre - but both are nominal. One manufacturer's 700c (the 'c' is just a code letter) is ever so slightly different to the next and can be either under or oversize for your rims. Bewildered? Stick around, because to add to the confusion, there are also various options for tyres to be under or over-width, with benefits as well as disadvantages dependent on what sort of cycling you intend to do - wider tyres are aimed at comfort, while narrower are designed for speed.

Short-haul touring is best done on 32mm plus wide tyres, preferably heavier ones to soak up the extra wear and tear. For longer trips, when you'll carry more weight, use at least 35mm tyres with treads suitable for both tarmac and track i.e. semi-slick or trekking. Finding that optimum combination of width and tread pattern will affect your comfort and speed over any length of journey and, again, this is governed by the type of surface you'll be cycling on and the amount of gear you decide to take.

The tyre's size is usually stated on the sidewall - e.g. 700x38c, where the 700 refers to the diameter in mm and 38 to its width (sometimes its imperial equivalent is added in brackets). There is also an ISO number (International Standards Organisation) next to it, which not only further clouds the issue, but hasn't really managed to standardise anything. This number, which on a 700x38c tyre should read '38-622', gives the tyre's width in the first two digits, together with the metric diameter of the tyre at its inside edge (the bead) in the other three digits. For 26 inch tyres, the 'bead' diameter is 599 and, in both cases, it's important to have the right size inner tube fitted - too large an inner tube can, in exceptional cases, force the tyre off the rim.

Many 700c touring tyres can now be bought (at a slightly increased cost) with 'puncture protection', eliminating punctures caused by smaller nuisances such as splinters and thorns. The usual method is via a thin strip of a substance called 'Kevlar', which runs along the crown of the tyre cover. There is also a DIY version - a protective band placed between inner tube and outer cover, but this is awkward to install and can sometimes slip, creating more problems than it solves.

Valves, like tyres, also come in two common sizes - the more slender Presta used on 700c tubes and the American Schraeder, usually seen on 26 inch tubes. Presta valves have a screw and pin mechanism, which is opened when inflating the tyre with a standard bike pump. Schraeders can be inflated directly by using the air-line at your local garage. The correct pressure limit is yet another important piece of information embossed on the tyre's wall, and this is critical in maintaining good road performance and reducing tread wear and sidewall

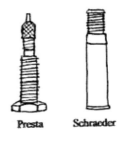

Presta   Schraeder

Valves

damage. To get it right, you can either use a tyre gauge or invest in a calibrated track pump. Knowing your ideal tyre pressure not only saves you energy when riding, but also lessens the chance of getting a puncture.

All things considered, the perfect compromise for a touring tyre is a puncture protected 700x35c (35-622). This can be pumped up to a reasonably high pressure, so reducing rolling resistance, but is also wide enough to take some of the bumps out of the road. With a tread pattern blending a central road strip and an outer track grip, this will give a comfortable and efficient ride on short to medium tours. For longer expeditions, you can take on a 38mm wide tyre to help cope with the load, the increased distance and the variations in surface that you're bound to meet along the way.

Popular 700c brands are Maxxis, Schwalbe and Continental, which all offer a good range of widths and tread patterns for touring bikes.

Wheels

Much of what has been said about tyres also applies to the touring bike's wheelset. The 'wheelset' refers to the rims, spokes and hubs, and the ideal tourer needs a robust and reliable set that won't buckle, break or seize when tested under the strain and the punishment of a long journey.

As with all bike parts, you can spend a fortune on hand built wheels oozing the sort of technology that will make your head (as well as your bike) spin. A moderately priced tourer, however, will already possess the wheels to do the job - stainless steel spokes, sturdy hubs and 700c alloy rims. Although usually associated with mountain and commuter bikes, some touring machines have recently transferred allegiance to 26 inch wheels - the argument being that they are smaller, wider-rimmed and therefore stronger. From the purist's viewpoint, however, modern 700c wheels are a more than adequate match in terms of strength and, allied to a sound touring tyre, have similar qualities to the 26 incher. Good 700c rims should be double-walled for strength and of 'touring specific' width, capable of accepting tyres from 32mm to 38mm. Hubs should be designed to take the added weight and have quick release mechanisms. Spokes should number at least 36 (36H - where 'H' stands for 'holes') - on some bikes you can get a different number of spokes, back and front; e.g. 40H rear and 36H front to help manage the greater burden on the back wheel.

Mavic, WTB, Alex and Shimano are amongst the best 700c rims found on touring cycles and, together with Shimano hubs and 36 spokes (front and rear), would make a good combination for your wheel set.

Brakes

There are three main designs of brake in use on modern bikes. The least harsh and exceptionally reliable dual-pivot calliper brake is found primarily on racing bikes. Although this is just an upgraded version of the old-fashioned side pull system, titanium bodies and carbon fibre pad holders can ratchet up the cost of a decent set to over £250.

For mountain bikes and, inevitably, spilling over into its town and country cousins, the trend is towards mechanical disc brakes and the more expensive option of hydraulic disc brakes. On top of the range 'hard-tails', the hydraulic brake proves extremely consistent, even in the wet, and gives increased stopping power where it's needed. The downside is that all disc brakes are difficult to service and maintain yourself, resulting in costly trips to the local bike shop.

Most touring bikes use cantilever V-brakes (as do many mountain bikes and hybrids). Far easier to fix, maintain and adjust than hydraulic discs and just as efficient as mechanical discs, they are the obvious choice for long distance cycling. The other half of the marriage making up the brakeset - the brake pad - is, again, easier to replace and set on a V-brake system than on disc brakes.

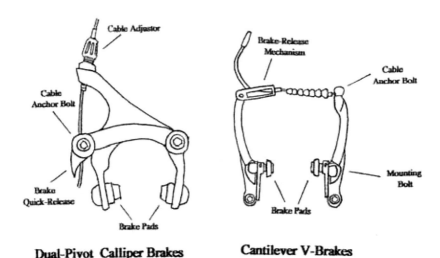

Dual-Pivot Calliper Brakes   **Cantilever V-Brakes**

Excellent V-brakes with that 'sure stop' ability, so important when carrying the heavier loads demanded on long tours, are made by Avid and Shimano.

Gears

Apart from 'fixed-wheel' and single-speeds, there are basically two systems - the derailleur system and hub gears. Modern hub gears were developed from the 3-speed Sturmey-Archer model and can have anything from 4 to 8 cogs built into the rear wheel hub. In addition, there is an external sprocket onto which the chain runs, helping to cut down on wear and reduce friction. With a reasonably wide range of ratios and (being enclosed) virtually maintenance free, they are the ideal solution for the mechanically bereft and those who don't want to get involved in cycle hardware. When things do go wrong, however, it's a job for the expert, and if the wheel needs changing for any reason, so does the hub gear.

In contrast, the derailleur system is an engineering nightmare that, theoretically, shouldn't work as well as it does. On the plus side, it's fixable, light, and cheap and has a large and variable range of gears. Cogs can be interchanged and modified to suit any terrain or incline - great for mountain biking, racing and touring.

Derailleur Gear System

By definition, the derailleur itself is a 'mechanism for moving the chain from one sprocket (cog) to another' - i.e. it 'derails' the chain off the cog. Two such devices, worked by cables, are used to change gear on two sets of cogs, and the complete system involves a front 'chainset' (double or triple) and a rear 'freewheel' cassette of up to 9 gears. With a chain linking front to rear, controlled by the derailleurs, a variety of speeds is available, although certain combinations of back and front gears are inevitably duplicated.

This relationship between speed and gear can be thought of as being similar to that of a car's. For steep inclines we would normally select low gears (1st or 2nd); on the flat we would use high gears (3rd, 4th or 5th). With a bike's derailleur system, there are typically 24 gears available (3 front x 8 rear). 1st gear is found by using the smallest front cog with the largest rear. Conversely, 24th gear uses the largest front with the smallest rear. So for inclines, we would retain the smallest front cog and flick through the 8 rear cogs to suit whatever degree of slope confronts us. On the flat or downhill, we choose the largest front cog and shift through the 8 rear cogs as required and as your speed picks up. The middle front cog tends to be the one most often used; i.e. for normal cycling conditions on town or country roads, when you're in no particular hurry.

The chainset and freewheel cassette are characterised by their 'teeth number'. For example, 48/38/28T states the number of teeth on the 3 front cogs and 12-30T/8speed describes a rear cassette of 8 cogs increasing from 12 to 30 teeth. The overall 'gear range' is found by adding the front and rear ranges of teeth together. 48/38/28T has a spread of 20 and 12-30T has a spread of 18; so, the total gear range is 20 + 18 = 38.

Most racing bikes have a double chainset with, perhaps, a gear range of 22. A tourer will have a range of about 40 (incorporating a low 'first' gear) to assist with the weight carried and the variations in incline, and would use a triple chainset and 8/9 speed cassette. This allows for an efficient 'cadence' (rate of pedalling) of around 60 to 70 revs per minute, regardless of terrain and wind conditions. For mountain bikes and similar machines, the gear range would be smaller.

There are also different types of gear shift. Popular on some cheaper bikes is the 'gripshift' mechanism, which changes gear by twisting the handlebar grip. The majority of conventional levers are now 'indexed', giving fixed positions for corresponding gears, both front and rear. This has completely eliminated the problem of 'feeling' for the correct cog (usual on older machines) by using two push levers to travel up and down the gears, one at a time. An extremely positive and efficient 'shifter', the indexed gear change is definitely the best option for a touring bike.

Championed by the Japanese company, Shimano, the SIS (Shimano Index System) has several commercial trade-names such as 'Rapidfire' and 'EZ-Fire', and are the most common make of gear shift. Likewise, the market for derailleur mechanisms, chainsets, etc has also been largely cornered by Shimano, with SRAM and Campagnolo providing other quality alternatives.

Indexed Gear Shifters

Saddle

Often the butt of jokes (pardon the pun), the most sensitive point of contact on your bike is your bum. The saddle is, without doubt, the one really personal item of cycling equipment and one that demands due consideration. Some people become so attached, they hang on to their old saddles, even when they buy a new bike.

There are, unfortunately, no absolutes in 'saddle advice' - just recommendations. The initial temptation is a wide, soft seat with springs, which paradoxically will leave you nursing saddle sores and walking like John Wayne. 'Soft' absorbs energy over distance and produces too much friction; the same applies to huge springs. 'Wide' will again cause soreness after hours in the saddle by becoming hot and sweaty because of the larger surface area. As a rough guide, reasonably hard and narrow (to fit the natural shape between your legs) with a little padding beneath a mock leather/chamois cover is good for touring. Beyond that, it's a case of trying out various saddles to discover which feels best. Remember, everybody's rear end is shaped differently and for the fairer sex, the rules are different again.

Other critical comfort factors involve 'setting' your saddle correctly - fixing the tilt so that it's horizontal and lifting your seatpost to the right height can make all the difference (see Size and Fit on page 46). Having done this, if you want to take some of the sting out of uneven road surfaces, a shock-absorbent (suspension) seatpost might be the solution. This can be adjusted to harden or soften the damper unit and acts directly on the saddle rails rather than on the saddle itself.

For tourers, more expensive doesn't necessarily mean better. Super-lightweight materials and titanium rails (which can cost a fortune) don't make much sense when your bike bags are groaning with wet weather gear, spares and overnight kit. A modern mid-priced saddle, slightly padded and tuned for longer rides is the answer, but only after you've made sure that it fits your particular anatomy. Female-specific saddles are designed a little wider and shorter to protect the 'sit bones' in the pelvic area, with strategically placed gel inserts and grooves. Good makes for all are WTB, Specialized and Selle-Italia, but if you're willing to 'break it in', you could do worse than invest in a real leather Brooks Special.

Brooks B17 saddle   Post-Moderne suspension seatpost

Pedals

What type of pedal you decide to push is down to the bike, the ride and individual preference. Clipless pedals are ultra-efficient because they allow the pedal to be pulled up as well as pushed down. The interlocking of shoe cleat and pedal does take some getting used to though, and certain makes of shoe can be awkward to walk in, but as with everything, it comes with practice. For road racing and cross-country mountain biking they are the perfect choice, albeit an expensive one. Other issues with clipless pedals involve the limited lateral movement of the foot when locked in. Everyone walks (and cycles) with a slightly different foot angle and, if this is restricted, problems with your knee joints can follow. Good clipless pedals do cater for this by having some degree of rotation, but care must be taken when adjusting shoe cleats to match foot angle.

If you don't like the idea of being 'permanently' attached to your bike, and you want something more efficient than standard resin pedals, you could try metal ones with toe clips. Also, a good alternative to the flexible steel toe-clip with straps is a rigid, strapless clip. Made from hardened plastic, they are tough and reliable, and easy to slot your feet into - a sensible choice for those of us who don't want to use straps or cleated cycling shoes, but need that extra push up hills.

Modern 'touring' pedals capable of taking toe-clips are usually double-sided and have steel cages and axles, alloy bodies and smooth bearings. Good brands of toe-clip compatible pedals are Wellgo and MKS and, together with a pair of rigid clips, would set you back no more than £25.

Wellgo pedal   Rigid toe-clip

Handlebars

Along with saddle and pedals, the handlebars take the other share of the cyclist's bodyweight. The shape of the bars and how they're set are not only important for comfort but also for safety and, as with all things, it's a bit of a compromise. A certain amount of weight distribution on the handlebars makes for improved steering and braking; too much forward bodyweight hurts your back, neck and wrists and numbs your hands.

Drop bars give plenty of options to vary hand position and therefore body position. This enables the rider to make adjustments when faced with changes in terrain, incline and wind conditions. Lowering your grip gives better aerodynamics to help cheat the wind - holding the top of the bars leaves you sitting more comfortably for cycling on the flat; this is why touring bikes have traditionally always used drop-style handlebars.

Hybrids have flat bars which, although not completely straight, can only provide very limited hand movement. For this reason, it's a good idea to add bar-ends to give that extra option of hold when spending long hours in the saddle. Other improvements, such as adjusting stem height and fitting cushioned grips, make the flat bar more acceptable for touring.

If you can't get on with drop bars and you feel that straight bars are too restrictive, there's yet another alternative - 'butterfly' shaped trekking bars. Although all three shapes are available on modern tourers, some cyclists maintain that the butterfly bar embodies many of the virtues of the other two. It certainly gives a variety of hand positions and, with an angle adjustable stem, comfort is greatly improved regardless of body shape or changes in riding position. Peripheral equipment (brake levers and gear levers) can again be positioned on the butterfly bar to wherever you feel is the most accessible.

Whatever the choice, all bars these days are made of lightweight alloy, conforming to strict safety standards regarding strength, and coming in varying thicknesses and widths to suit all hand sizes and body frames.

'Butterfly' Trekking Bars

Racks and Mudguards

On a long trip, your luggage is best balanced over the complete length of the bike by using rear and front pannier racks. This gives the ideal set-up of two rear panniers and another two at the front, with the option of a bar bag if needed - loads of space for your gear, and producing predictable steering and braking.

Good aluminium racks should be substantial and well anchored (see page 34). Front racks come in high and low-mounted versions. The 'low-rider' rack is preferable, as it drops the centre of gravity on the front wheel and improves handling. One either side of the bike, they are normally fixed half-way up the front forks (via bosses) with eyelets at the bottom of the forks providing anchorage. The rear rack is attached to bosses and eyelets on the seatstays, and should be long enough and wide enough to allow panniers to be attached without too much effort. Most touring bikes will already be fitted with racks (certainly at the back); if not, any decent cycle shop will order them for you.

Much scoffed at by the mountain bike fraternity (who use silly little strap-on things), the full-length mudguard is a must for the tourer. Chromoplastic guards with stainless steel stays and plastic-capped safety ends are lightest and best. Again touring bike frames will have plenty of clearance to accept the correct width of mudguard, whereas some hybrids might struggle. As with wheels and tyres, mudguards are dimension specific, so get a 700x36-44c pair, which will cover any larger width tyre. Make sure, also, that there are stays on each mudguard (two either side).

As examples of good quality bikes (tourer and hybrid) that wouldn't cost a fortune and incorporate much of what has just been discussed, I've chosen two models made by the same manufacturer. This not only illustrates how one maker differentiates between these two types of machine, but also how many of the parts mentioned in the specifications are common to both.

Tourer

Specifications

Make: Dawes

Model: Kara Kum Touring Cycle - weight 14.5 Kg

Frame: Light alloy touring frame (17", 19", 21")

Forks: Unicrown chromoly with low-rider rack bosses

Tyres: Schwalbe Silento touring tyres - 700x38c(38-622) -
           puncture protected - reflective stripe

Wheels: Cross country 700c - WTB black alloy, dual duty
           rims - Shimano quick-release alloy hubs - stainless
           steel spokes (36H)

Brakes: Shimano V-brakes - Tektro brake levers

Gears: Shimano Deore 27 speed - Rapidfire indexed gear
               shift - Shimano triple chainset 48/38/26T - Shimano rear
               cassette 11-32T/9 speed

Saddle: Dawes Comfort touring saddle

Seatpost: Adjustable suspension post - Kalloy damper unit

Pedals: Wellgo with steel cage and alloy body - rigid open
               toe-clips

Handlebars: Comfort trekking bar - 'butterfly' style - alloy

Stem: Alloy quill - angle adjustable

Bike Rack: Dawes alloy tubular - integral reflector

Mudguards: Full chromoplastic - double stainless safety stays

When discussing the merits of the hybrid bike for touring purposes, we
have to look at a specific type - not just anything that happens to have a
hybrid frame in an increasingly widening market of city and utility bikes.
From its classic definition of being the marriage of a mountain bike frame
and a road bike wheelset, the touring hybrid is a machine that is geared to
take on hills, saddled for comfort and built to carry pannier racks and
mudguards.
    The frame itself, being closer to that of a mountain bike than a tourer,
has a top tube with a slightly greater slope, but still retains a relaxed
geometry, so essential for long distance cycling. Strong 700c wheels are
double-walled and wide enough to accept 35mm tyres, following the
semi-slick touring pattern of road centre and track outer tread. Composite
or chromoly forks, V-brakes, Shimano indexed gearing, suspension

seatpost and bosses for front as well as rear racks complete the picture - all the features of the tourer, apart from that extra lick of speed on the flat. With one or two modifications, such as attaching bar-ends for added hand positions and fitting toe-clips, the hybrid bike is ready for the road.

Hybrid

Specifications

Make: Dawes

Model: Sonoran Trekking Bike

Frame: Light alloy hybrid frame - Gents (18", 20", 22") -
            Ladies (16", 18")

Forks: Unicrown hi-tensile steel with low-rider rack bosses

Tyres: Kenda Khan touring tyres - 700x35c(35-622)

Wheels: 700c alloy, dual duty rims - Shimano quick-release alloy
             hubs - stainless steel spokes (36H)

Brakes: Shimano V-brakes - Tektro brake levers

Gears: Shimano Alvio 24 speed - EZ-fire indexed gear shift
             - Shimano triple chainset 48/38/28T - Shimano rear
             cassette 11-23T/8speed

Saddle: Dawes Comfort saddle

Seatpost: Adjustable suspension post

Pedals: Non-slip alloy

Handlebars: Flat 620mm trekking bar with comfort grips

Stem: Alloy quill - angle adjustable

Bike Rack: Alloy - integral reflector

Mudguards: Full chromoplastic - double safety stays

4

Buying your Bike - Your Choice

There's a two-wheeled match somewhere out there just for you. Do your research, take advice and keep your options open.

Before looking in detail at the different ways you can buy a bike, the listings on the next page may help to provide an insight into a sample of tourers and hybrids that could be used as a starting point for researching your own dream machine. I've limited prices to an affordable level and completely avoided the cheaper end of the market, but, as we are so often told, you only get what you pay for and touring/hybrid bikes are no exception. You've got to think in terms of £350 plus to get something strong enough, light enough and well-equipped enough to do the journey. At the same time, I've tried to keep costs below £700 and, by doing your own leg work before passing over your hard-earned cash, bargains can be found. 'Recommended retail price' doesn't necessarily mean that's what you actually pay.

No matter how you end up buying your bike, whether it's from a local shop, the Internet, an auction or the small ads, try to spend to the limit of your budget. The temptation to save some money by getting a much cheaper, second choice will lead to regret and might even kill off your enthusiasm for cycling altogether by seeing it as just that - second best. Having said that, don't forget to allow for essentials such as helmet, locks, lights, etc in your overstretched budget.

Next, make sure you research the market thoroughly. Look at cycle magazines, check out reviews on the Internet and search manufacturers' websites. Have a chat with the guy at the bike shop, but be aware that he will probably be pushing the tourer in his shop window rather than giving an independent overview.

	Raleigh Royal	Dawes Kara Kum	Cannondale Trekking Ultra	Claude Butler Regent	Trek Allant	Ridgeback Horizon	Dawes Sonoran
Type	Tourer	Tourer	Hybrid	Tourer	Hybrid	Tourer	Hybrid
RRP	£459	£629	£699	£499	£350	£499	£350
Frame	Cromoly 50-60cm	Alloy 17"-21"	Alloy 48-61cm	Alloy 48-57cm	Alloy 18"-22"	Alloy 52-60cm	Alloy 18"-22"
Forks	Cromoly	Cromoly	Cromoly	Cromoly	Cromoly	Carbon	Steel
Wheels	Dual Duty Alloy	Dual Duty WTB	Dual Duty Mavic	Dual Duty Rigida	Alloy Matrix	Alloy Alex	Dual Duty Alloy
Tyres	700x32c Maxxis	700x38c Schwalbe	700x35c Schwalbe	700x35c Kenda	700x35c	700x25c Contal	700x35c Kenda
Gears	Shimano 24 Speed	Shimano 27 Speed	Shimano 27 Speed	Shimano 24 Speed	Shimano 21 Speed	Shimano 27 Speed	Shimano 24 Speed
Brakes	Tektro V	Shimano V	Shimano V	Tektro V	Shimano V	Tektro V	Shimano V
Saddle	Avenir Tour	Dawes Comfort	Selia Royal	CB Comfort	Touring	Touring	Dawes Comfort
Bars	Drop	Butterfly	Flat	Drop	Flat	Drop	Flat
Extras	Mudguards, Racks	Mudguards, Racks	Mudguards, Racks	Mudguards, Racks	Mudguards, Racks	Mudguards	Mudguards, Racks

Lastly, don't be blinkered into chasing one particular model - have alternatives in mind around the price you can afford, and get to know their virtues and drawbacks. Go for comparable lightness and strength, specification and accessories. Recognise which bikes can be easily modified to suit your purpose if your dream model is way beyond financial reach. Above all else, having taken into account market analysis, affordability and availability, ask yourself the question, 'Am I 99 per cent happy with what I'm about to buy?' One per cent uncertainty is acceptable - an impulse purchase usually spells disaster.

The Bike Shop

In an ideal world, buying your new bike from a local independent cycle shop or chain is the answer. You get convenience, personal attention from knowledgeable staff, practical help with size and fitting and, usually, a free initial service. You can try out your preferred model and look at other options in the same price range. Pedals, saddles, handlebars and

stems can all be adjusted or swapped for something that will make the bike a better fit. Even if the right size bike isn't in stock, it can easily be ordered and quickly delivered.

Deals can also be done. You'll already know the bottom line from your research in magazines and on your PC and this information can be used in negotiating the final price. This doesn't mean you'll get it at bargain basement cost - your local shop is not a mass retailer and has to look at its overheads and profit margins. But they might just throw in accessories such as lights, mudguards, etc. on top of their own discount. Another useful tip is that most dealers make their annual change of models in the autumn, in time for the coming Christmas season. This provides an excellent opportunity for picking up a reduced 'older' model, which might only mean taking on last year's colour or forfeiting the odd component improvement. So, if you're not too bothered about it clashing with your new lime-green cycling outfit or missing out on the very latest in bell technology - great!

Lastly, it's important to remember that the advantages of having a good local bike shop for advice, buying spares and bike servicing can sometimes outweigh the temptation to get a few pounds knocked off the retail price elsewhere. Using a mail order company or the Internet doesn't always work out the cheapest in the long run.

Buying Online

Paradoxically described as a 'gold-mine' and a 'mine-field' of information, the Internet can hold both promise and dread for the unsuspecting cycling googler. Most sites are straightforward

enough - manufacturers, retailers and other outlets selling new bikes, spares, clothing, books, etc. Some retailers sell their wares exclusively through the Internet, one of which recently earned a 'best bike' award in a national cycling magazine. Big chains have their own websites and there are really good deals to be found here, especially in the 'last year's model' category. Others, however, such as mail order companies pushing self-assembly cycles delivered in flat-packs, are largely unknown quantities and the purchaser has to put his trust in the description given.

Not all online buys are doubtful. Chainreactioncycles.com is an international website dealing in well known names such as Giant and Scott. Wiggle.co.uk is another mail order firm that is particularly good for hybrid bikes, often selling 'ex-demo' models (GT, Kona, Giant) at 20-

25% discount off list prices.

If you're looking for a second-hand bike, a wide and varied array is available on eBay. When I visited the site, there were 116 touring cycles for auction, including Cannondale, Trek and Raleigh, as well as tandems and touring recumbents. You get a photograph and a brief description, but in the end, it comes down to your own good judgement (or lack of it) - satisfaction and disappointment can be had in equal measure.

The Auction

As with bikes bought via the Internet, buying at auction is also fraught with danger. Perhaps, the worst of both worlds is the auction website, where 'buyer beware' holds added significance. Whether it's second-hand or a brand new flat-pack, you're inevitably dealing with something totally unseen. Bargains can be had, but it's  more than likely you'll be disappointed, and getting your money back is often daunting.

The auction 'proper' is a better bet. At least you can look over the stock, even if you can't physically try it out. If you don't know much about bikes yourself, take someone along who does - that way you won't end up with a 'shed' with buckled wheels, a seized crank and a cracked frame. The auctioneer's idea of rideaway condition might mean anything from something approaching the truth to 'it falls to pieces after cycling ten yards'.

Have in mind good makes and models of the type of bike you're after. If it's a tourer, opt for a modern lightweight with modern components. Try to spot any broken parts and assess the cost of replacement; look for grime and rust, which will indicate the bike's age and/or lack of maintenance. Finally, go with a set budget and stick to it - yet another good reason for taking someone with you just in case you're tempted to pay a king's ransom for the object of your desire. Always be prepared to walk away if nothing fits the bill.

Auctions fall into one of two categories. Your local auction house may hold a bike sale at intervals during the year. You'll have the opportunity to view (and examine closely) what's on offer prior to the auction date and make a mental shortlist of possibilities. At the same time, you can register at the auction office and pay your deposit (refundable). On the actual day, give things time to warm up. It's often the more popular 'mountain type' bikes that go through first and these are usually snapped up by dealers. If you've spotted a good tourer, chances are you'll be in a minority of bidders and could well walk away with a real bargain.

Police auctions run along similar lines. Simply ask at your local police station or visit 'bumblebeeauctions.co.uk' to find the next and nearest. The rule for lost and stolen cycles is that they remain in police custody for 6 weeks, after which they're put up for sale. With proceeds going to charity, the bikes are normally kept at the local lost property office and then auctioned off regularly throughout the year.

In all auctions, there's usually a 10% auctioneer's fee to be paid by the purchaser. There are no guarantees or warranties of safety and roadworthiness - that's down to you. It's your responsibility once you've wheeled your bike out of the room.

The Second-hand Market

The second-hand bike, regardless of where you source it, has its own obvious pitfalls. These apply equally to online purchases, a buy from an auction or one from the small ads/shop window. Oddly, perhaps the best bet, if you're fortunate enough to strike lucky, is the chap up the road who's upgrading his old tourer/hybrid and selling it on for a snip. If we take that possibility out

of the equation, then there are a few basic rules to follow when looking for a good second-hand machine.

Frame: The bedrock of any good bike is its frame. Normal wear and tear is to be expected, but avoid a frame (or forks) that's bent or damaged. Feel under the top tube and down tube for tell-tale cracks in the paintwork, which might indicate a weak point caused by impact. If the seatpost is rusted, it's likely to be seized in the seat tube and impossible to adjust. Don't buy anything with an obviously neglected frame that's been badly scarred or dented.

Steering: The headset can be tested by applying the front brake and pushing the bike forward. If the bike rocks, either the headset is out of adjustment or the bearings are damaged. Having tightened the nut on the headset, test it again by lifting the bike and gently turning the steering as far as it will go - any grating could indicate a pitted headset, which would mean replacement.

Wheels: 'Truing' a slightly buckled wheel is easy enough if no spokes are missing. Replacing a broken or missing spoke is better done at the bike shop, where the wheel can be aligned at the same time. Look for excessive wear on rims and test for undue play in the hubs by wobbling the wheel sideways. A worn tyre with the canvass showing through is a definite pointer to general neglect.

Drivetrain: This incorporates the rear cassette, chainset, derailleurs, bottom bracket and chain. In operation, the cogs should engage smoothly up and down the gears. Any slight wear in the teeth is acceptable and if the chain is catching on the front derailleur, this can usually be resolved by adjustment. If the chain is rusted or stretched it will need replacing, which probably means replacing the rear cassette as well, and this cost has to be taken into account. Test the bottom bracket by rocking the cranks sideways. In cases of excessive movement, this becomes another expensive fix.

Others: As far as brakes, saddle, mudguards, pedals and racks are concerned, it's just a matter of checking that they work/are serviceable. For any second-hand bike, you may well replace the saddle and also renew various parts over time and as required.

When it comes to looking over your prospective second-hand purchase, make sure you take a tape measure to confirm its size (which is covered in detail below) and a torch for closer inspection of cogs, hubs, wheel rims, etc. Road test it to see if it 'feels' the part and that gears are smooth and brakes are efficient. Try to make a mental costing of parts that need renewing and whether or not it's a DIY option or a job for the expert. Don't be lured into buying a bike that, after estimating your outlay for repairs, might come to almost as much as a shiny new one.

Size and Fit

Second-hand or brand new, there are three basic elements to size and fit. The first, manufacturer's size, refers to the frame of the bike, and is the length of the seat tube from top to bottom (i.e. to the centre of the crank). Given either in inches or centimetres (1 inch = 2.54cm), it is crucial to get this measurement right before attempting the fine tuning of 'fit'. For the size to be correct there must be 1 to 2 inches of clearance in standover height. So, for a hybrid or touring top tube, when you straddle the frame, there should be at least 1 inch between the tube (at its mid-point) and your crotch. If there isn't, not only will the frame prove to be oversize, but it could also cause untold damage if you happen to come off your seat in an emergency stop.

   Having bought the right size bike, next come considerations of comfort - how the bike 'fits' your particular body shape. Saddle type (which has already been touched on) is a critical factor where comfort is concerned. Its tilt, fore-and-aft position and height are the other essentials. If a saddle is badly adjusted, legs, arms, back, neck and bum are bound to suffer.

   Tilt should be horizontal (parallel to the road). Some books recommend a slight forward tilt, others a slight backward tilt. Flat is best for touring - this takes your weight centrally, which is how the saddle was designed in the first place.

Loosening the clamp to affect tilt also allows the saddle to be moved backwards and forwards along its rails i.e. fore-and-aft adjustment. The correct lateral position is found with cranks set horizontally ('quarter to three'). Using a wall for balance and seated comfortably with the balls of your feet on the pedals, a plumb line should then drop accurately from the hollow on your forward knee-cap to the centre of the forward pedal axle. This means that your weight is distributed evenly when cycling.

Saddle Fore-and-aft Adjustment

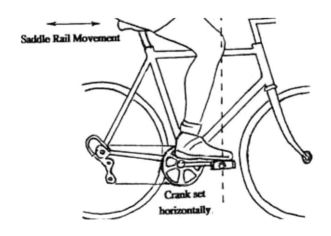

For saddle height to be properly adjusted, first set the cranks in line with the seat tube. Place your heel on the lower pedal and slowly pedal backwards. If the saddle height is correct, your leg should be straight at the bottom of the stroke, with just the slightest sense of wobble on your saddle. More pronounced than this, means the saddle is too high and can be moved using the release bolt on the seat tube. Don't forget to make sure your saddle is also in line with the top tube (not twisted sideways) and that the 'minimum insertion' mark on the seatpost isn't visible.

Saddle Height Adjustment

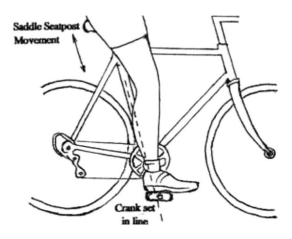

The third part to cycling comfort is handlebar adjustment. Whether it's a tourer or a hybrid, get the bars that feel most comfortable for you - right style, right width, and right thickness for your hands. The handlebar height is fixed by loosening the expander bolt in the stem and, ideally, setting the bars level with the saddle. For drop or butterfly bars, this means raising the 'flat' section of the bars to the same height as the saddle and, if the top part of the stem is angle adjustable, moving that as well to further fine tune your reach. Once adjusted, brake and gear levers can be moved to make sure that wrists are straight when braking and gear shifters are within easy reach.

Obviously, everyone's body frame is different and won't always conform to the perfect average. In the end, you will have to tweak all these positions to best suit your particular form until you find the point at which you're most comfortable. With any minor adjustments though, make them one at a time and in small increments, testing them out on the road before making the next.

So, with the right size bike frame, plus saddle and bars positioned for touring, your back, arms and top tube should theoretically form an equilateral triangle when viewed from the side. You should feel perfectly relaxed when cycling and be able to view everything ahead without straining your neck. The balance between saddle and handlebars will leave your back fairly straight and, at the same time, will avoid placing too much weight on your wrists. You should now be able to tick off the miles and the hours with optimum comfort and perfect cycling efficiency.

5

Biking Accessories - Touring Needs

These are the bits you simply can't leave home without. They'll keep you safe, secure and will ease your journey from A to B.

Helmets

There is a very good argument for wearing a cycling helmet - in low-impact accidents, it will shield your head (and brain) by absorbing the force of your fall. In a high-speed crash, it affords only limited protection, but regardless of the severity of the spill, the helmet undoubtedly offers a better physical safeguard than if you're not wearing one. Controversially, not everyone is in agreement with this rationale. The anti-helmet camp quotes one piece of research which theorises that vehicle drivers treat helmet wearing cyclists with slightly less regard than their more vulnerable 'naked' counterparts - i.e. if you don't have a helmet, you somehow need to be given a wider berth. Most people, however, would see this as merely clouding the issue.

   In many countries, wearing a helmet is compulsory; in Britain it isn't. If you do decide to do the sensible thing, there's a wide choice to pick from and one which will suit every pocket. Again, you get what you pay for. Top of the range helmets can cost up to £100, although in terms of safety, the extra money doesn't necessarily buy you extra protection - just better and lighter technology. A good mid-range helmet for touring, such as Giro, Bell or Abus, should set you back no more than £40. Check the safety rating on the inside of the helmet - BSI (British Standards Institute), ASTM, CEN and Snell all represent different countries' safety certification and the more stickers it has, the better. Should you be unlucky enough to fall and damage your helmet, then replace it. Some manufacturers even offer a subsidised replacement service for new ones, so there's no real excuse.

Finally, note that helmets come in all sizes and fittings, universally designed for both genders. There are also separate female-specific models aimed at the smaller (and prettier) head.

Giro Indicator helmet

Locks

The helmet provides safety for your head - the lock provides safety for your bike. Bearing in mind that bike crime is largely opportunist, an unlocked cycle, wherever it's left, takes literally just seconds to steal. Although any sort of lock will inevitably delay that process, if you leave your bike in an 'out of the way' spot, you're only helping the thief by giving him more time to tamper. Always leave it in sight - always fasten it to something substantial and immovable - always use your locks to best effect.

There are three main types of lock in common use; the cable (or chain) lock, the D lock and the immobiliser. The cable lock is light, portable and cheap, and presents a good visible deterrent. It can be passed through frame, wheels and saddle cage to hold those bits that are more readily detached and any 'exploitable' slack is easy to take up. Chain locks, which are made of steel links running through a fabric cover, are much heavier and less flexible, although they are stronger and prove difficult to cut.

D locks (or U locks) are fashioned from hardened steel and built to resist a more determined attack, but are relatively expensive - anything from £50 to £150. They are, however, one of the best and safest locks you can buy, consisting of a solid round-sectioned bar that fits neatly into an integral locking mechanism. Usually rated gold, silver or bronze on a 'sold secure' certificate, quality increases with price, with Abus and Kryptonite being the names to look for.

In low risk situations, an immobiliser can be used. Ideal for short stops where your bike is in sight, it can be fitted to the frame and looped around the wheel. More of a visual prevention really, it is fairly easy to break and should be used in conjunction with a conventional lock.

For both touring and commuting, the best configuration would be a D lock attached to seat tube and rear wheel, interlocked with a cable tied round the frame and front wheel. Fastened to something solid, such as railings or a lamppost, at least you're sending a message to potential thieves that you take security seriously. Abus have produced a 'partner pack' to this ends, which combines a Sinus 46 D lock and a Phantom cable lock for just over £60.

Abus Partner Pack Lock

Other common sense measures include buying insurance ('Cycleguard' is one of many specialist companies) and having your frame stamped with a security system such as Datatag. ID labels cost around £25 and are fed into the Police data base, but obviously this only works if your bike is recovered. On the plus side, it often earns a 10% discount on your insurance premium, and noting that over £30 million worth of bikes are stolen each year, these are undoubtedly options worth considering.

Pump

There's not a lot you can say about pumps. A modern frame fitting pump has attachments to fit both types of valve (Presta and Schraeder), as does the 'mini'. The latter is perhaps easier to pop in a bag and is therefore less vulnerable to opportunist theft. Some pumps have integral tyre gauges – some even come with CO_2 cartridges (ideal for the lame and the lazy). Once more, the choice is yours, with popular makes being Airtool, Blackburn and Topeak.

The Mini G Masterblaster, made by Topeak, is an 'all singing, all dancing' pump with an in-line pressure gauge, dual valve attachment and a lightweight body. At under £18, it's an excellent buy.

Topeak Mini G Masterblaster

Lighting System

Minimum legal lighting requirements and what might be considered effective lighting are two very different things. It is obviously important to be seen by other road users between the hours of sunset and sunrise, and the law states that you must have the following: a front light (white), a rear light (red), a rear red reflector and two amber reflectors on each pedal. Flashing LED (light emitting diode) lights are now acceptable, so long as the rate is between 60 and 240 flashes per minute. Add to this reflective strips on clothing and panniers and you can feel happy in the knowledge that you've done all you can to make yourself as visible as possible in the dark.

Effective lighting demands that your lights are not only good enough to be seen, but powerful enough to see the road ahead. You can spend literally hundreds on ultra-bright lighting sets or you can dip into the budget market of conventional battery models for just a few pounds. The most expensive lights include the rechargeable type which, unbelievably, can cost up to £700 - and that's just for the front! There are also dynamo powered lighting sets, which are either tyre or hub driven, but again, this is not a cheap investment.

Somewhere in-between the cheap and the steep will provide for a front light with a good direct beam and a strong rear light that can be seen at distance. A modern LED system adequately fits the bill and will operate for many hours before batteries need replacing. Manufacturers such as Bikehut, Cateye and Topeak all sell combination sets of front and rear lights for around £40.

The Cateye EL220 uses a 5 LED configuration that will illuminate the way ahead with a far reaching broad spread of light; combined with the LD150 rear light boasting three flashing modes, this compact set is perfect for commuting as well as long distance touring.

Cateye EL220 Lighting Set

Panniers

There are still the 'die-hards' who persist in carrying all their gear in a rucksack while cycling. Not only does this prove uncomfortable in the heat of summer, but it can also badly affect back, neck and shoulders. On top of this and no matter what the time of year, if you're wearing a backpack, the bike's handling can become less predictable and a sharp crosswind will leave you wobbling all over the road. For mountain bikers, it obviously makes perfect sense to set off with a Camelbak Mule or something similar strapped tightly to your body; not so for touring or longer commutes.

One alternative is the old-fashioned and very British institution of the saddlebag, which has made a comeback recently (now renamed the 'seatpack' or 'saddle day-bag'). For the tourer, however, they're seen as being more of a triumph of style over content than a really useful option. In the end, if you've got racks on your bike, panniers give you the ultimate flexibility for any length of journey. All permutations are possible, from a single rear pannier to the complete set - two front, two rear and a handlebar bag for your 'near to hand' essentials. So, certainly for longer trips, panniers remain a wonderfully efficient way of carrying your luggage.

From humble beginnings in the form of two large bags hooked on the back of a French baker's delivery bike ('pain' = bread), modern panniers are now both versatile and functional. Made from seam welded PVC or hard wearing Cordura/Nylon, most have useful compartments and pockets, and come in a range of capacities and styles. For touring, it's essential to buy good quality bags. Cordura panniers are tough and water resistant and they usually include high visibility covers, which give added waterproofing. Clever rack-release mechanisms have largely eliminated the problem of fumbling around with straps when you arrive at your destination and all decent makes have strong carrying handles.

Some bike manufacturers produce their own pannier sets and the market in general is flooded with many different brands. If you're considering a long tour, buying a full set of panniers would be sensible and would give your bike better balance. For shorter trips, two rear panniers and a handlebar bag might be best. Altura make good fabric bags with Dryline waterproofing, Klickfix rack fittings, reflective strips and carrying handles. Their range includes rear bags (17-28 litres each), front bags (16 litres each) and a bar bag with map case and shoulder strap (5 litres). Alternatively, there's nothing wrong with a mix and match combination of rear, front and bar bags using different manufacturers to suit your own particular capacity needs.

Altura Range of Panniers

Computer

Whether at home or abroad, accurate distance readings can be crucial when spending long days in the saddle; so you'll certainly need a reliable cycle computer on your travels.

If you're 'well into' all things electronic, as far as cycle computers are concerned, the world's your oyster. Multi-function, touch screen, hyper fast transmission, heart rate and cadence options, the lot. For someone like me who doesn't know his Bluetooth from any other type of filling, it's best to keep it as simple as possible - but definitely go for wireless. The Cateye Vectra 5 Wireless model is easy to set up and even easier to use, thanks to its single button operation. For £25 you get five useful functions (speed, time, odometer, overall distance and average speed) and I really can't imagine why you'd need any more.

Cateye Vectra 5

Tool Bag

Some tool bags can be fitted to the frame at the point where top tube meets seat tube, but these are usually too small to be useful. Travelling by bike demands a comprehensive array of tools (see next chapter) and a seat pack is a far better solution for holding those vital 'maintenance' bits and pieces.

Again, there are many different makes, but bearing in mind the weight it has to carry, buying a durable tool bag that will cope makes good sense. Topeak's classic Wedge Bag is tough with an expandable compartment, waterproof cover, strong zips and an ultra secure clip-on attachment. It's a simple job to fit the bracket to your saddle rails and the bag is roomy enough for all the essentials needed on a long trip. The Topeak Wedge Bag costs just £14.

Topeak Wedge Bag

Others

Water bottle and Cage: Fitting two cages/bottles (one on the down tube, one on the seat tube) is a must for touring. They're cheap and they're necessary, especially on longer tours in warmer climes, and when a basic cage and bottle costs just £6, it hardly represents a scandalous outlay. Options to spend a little more include aluminium insulated bottles to keep your water cool or you could even go for the Camelbak Podium bottle at £9, which eliminates that plastic aftertaste and also claims to keep your drink bacteria-free.

Bell: New bikes have bells fitted as a legal requirement. Not too useful on the open road, but indispensable for warning pedestrians when riding on busy cycle paths. Modern bells are light and cheap (£5), although I'm regularly reminded by one cycling friend that you can't beat an old-fashioned 'child-frightener'.

Kickstand: Easy to fit and costing around £10, a kickstand saves the frame's paintwork by avoiding that metal to metal contact. Even with a loaded bike (carefully balanced), it can still prove effective, but this doesn't mean you can sit on your machine at the same time. Available at all decent bike shops, you can also buy a twin-legged centre stand which has its own obvious advantages.

Mirror: Along with little flashing lights, having chrome plated mirrors can cause your bike to be mistaken for a disco. Normally, I wouldn't be in favour of fitting any sort of cycle mirror - they tend to suffer badly from vibration when mounted on your handlebars and are just two more sticky-out objects that are easily vandalised. However, a recently patented mirror called Bike-Eye has largely transformed that opinion. It gives a good long distance rear view, which makes it is easy to judge the speed of following traffic and, because of its design, can be fitted neatly to the down tube just above the front forks. This means that it is virtually vibration free and out of harm's way, and gives a perfectly clear reflection by exploiting the gap under the rider's leg.

The rider's view when the leg is in the optimum viewing position - freewheel for a few seconds if you need more time to observe

Bike-Eye Mirror

6

Bike Maintenance - Turning Wheels

The longer the trip, the more chance there is of something going wrong. Even if you're a mechanical novice, as a touring cyclist you'll need to be reasonably self-sufficient and fully armed with basic tools and spares. As always, the devil is in the detail.

Tools/spares

The following considerations have all been arrived at with modern touring/hybrid cycles very much in mind. The tools, the spares and the maintenance schedule detailed below are aimed specifically at these machines and also at the mechanical requirements of a medium length trip. Whatever you'll need for a week or two will be more than enough for a day or two, and probably (with a few additions) sufficient for an expedition.

Tools: It's worth investing in some decent bike tools. Although it represents yet another initial expense, once bought they're likely to last a lifetime. The list itself may seem extensive, but bear in mind that all these items will fit neatly into your tool bag along with your puncture repair kit and a rag.

Multitool

Small Phillips screwdriver
Small flat-head screwdriver
Multitool (shown above)
Spoke key

Tyre levers (plastic - 2)
Allen keys
Spanners (to fit your bike)
Small pliers
Chain breaker (screw type)
Small adjustable spanner

Spares: As with tools, your spares (and other bits) should fit compactly
into a plastic bag. The tyre will fold small and can then be taped.
Tyre (e.g. Continental Folding 700x37c(37-622))
Inner tubes (2)
Brake pads (4)
Spokes (4)
Chain links (2)
Brake cables (front and rear)
Gear cables (front and rear)
Cycle lock keys (spares)
Screws, bolts, nuts, washers, valve caps (to fit your bike)

Others: Puncture repair kit
Oil (light cycle oil)
Chain lubricant (self-cleaning wax lube)
Roll of electrical tape
Nylon ties (10 - various lengths)
Cleaning rag
Small tub of grease (film container)
Nylon strap with Klickfix fitting

For longer journeys and dependent on country, distance between towns
and, more importantly, whether or not cycle shops are commonplace, it
might be worth taking the following extras:-

Headset spanner
Cassette lockring tool (for removing freewheel)
Spare batteries for lighting set and cycle computer

The sum total weight of all the above tools and spares is approximately 2 Kg (5 lbs).

Now that you've acquired the tools and the spares, the next thing is the know-how. This section is not meant to turn you into a cycle mechanic overnight or to help the uninitiated complete a full service (that's a job for the bike shop and will be dealt with later in the chapter). But, with a little knowledge and equipment, you'll certainly be able to overcome simple problems on the road, which might otherwise delay your journey.

Perhaps the best advice initially is to know your bike. Basic preventative checks and adjustments - brakes, gears, wheels, tyres, lights and making sure that all nuts and bolts are tight is a start. Oiling moving parts (but not hubs and crank), lubricating chain and cables, and cleaning paintwork, wheels and exposed metal parts is also essential after a long ride or on a weekly basis (if commuting). Also, make sure you read the manufacturer's manual carefully and note its own recommendations on maintenance. After that, it's down to specifics.

Derailleur Gears

To understand the difficulties that occasionally crop up with the derailleur system, firstly consult photo1 to acquaint yourself with the various parts.

rear derailleur

front derailleur and chainset

cage pulley

Photo 1

Next, before making any adjustments to anything, degrease the two rear cage pulleys, the rear freewheel and the chain. Then lubricate the chain and pulleys with a wax lube such as 'Clean Ride' and check if the adjustment is still necessary.

Most gear problems involve poor/noisy chain movement from one cog to another, inability to find certain gears and the chain falling off either the front or back set of cogs (which can cause damage). Providing the chain, rear freewheel and front chainset aren't worn, all settings to solve these problems can be made quite quickly with a small screwdriver (Phillips or flat-head). At the same time, you have to accept that derailleur systems are not very tolerant of excessive wear, so if the chain is slipping badly on the rear freewheel, both chain and cassette will need renewing - you can't run a new chain on old cogs and vice versa. Be aware also, that after making your adjustments and testing all combinations of gears by 'pedalling' the system with your hand, further tinkering may be needed once you actually test your bike under strain on the road.

These crucial adjustments are basically (a) limiting the 'sideways' travel of the chain on both front and rear cogs and (b) ensuring clear and smooth gear change.

(a) (i) Front derailleur: the outer and inner limit screws (limiting the movement of the cage plates) are shown in photo 2. Facing forwards, the right-hand screw adjusts the limit of the outer cage plate and the left-hand screw limits the inner plate.

cage plates

limit screws   Photo 2

With the chain on the largest front chainring and the smallest rear cog, adjust the outer cage plate so that it's almost touching the chain (right-hand screw). Next, place the chain on the smallest front chainring and largest rear cog. Now turn the left-hand screw so that the inner cage plate is just over 1mm away from the chain. Finally, test the movement of the chain on all three front chainrings by shifting gear and turning the crank by hand.

(ii) Rear derailleur: The limit screws on the rear derailleur are located at the back of the derailleur and set vertically or at an angle (photo 3). The higher screw (H) limits the travel outwards towards the freewheel's smallest cog and the lower screw (L) adjusts the travel inwards to the largest cog. These adjustments eliminate problems in finding extreme gears and also, in avoiding the chain slipping off the cogs completely.

limit screws   Photo 3

To adjust the freewheel's outer limit, move the chain to the largest front chainring and smallest rear cog. Bending low and viewing it from the back, turn the higher screw so that the upper cage pulley is perfectly in line with the smallest cog. This sounds complicated, but is easy in practice (see photo 4).

So that the chain doesn't travel beyond its inner limit, position the chain on the smallest front chainring and largest rear cog. Now using the lower adjusting screw, visually line up the upper cage pulley with the largest cog. Double check that the chain can't overshoot that inner cog.

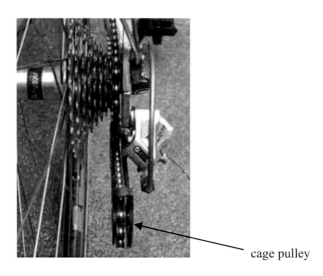

cage pulley

Photo 4

b) Cable adjustment: this usually requires a degree of trial and improvement and is only necessary if cables are slack or gear shift is noisy/erratic.

The cable to the front derailleur is adjustable at the gear lever by turning the plastic barrel. If the limit of adjustment has been reached and there's still not enough tension in the cable, undo the locking bolt at the cable end, adjust and retighten.

For the rear derailleur, set the chain on the middle front chainring and the second smallest rear cog. While turning the crank by hand, tighten the cable by winding the cable adjusting barrel anticlockwise (see photo 5). Stop tightening when the chain starts making a noise and test the tension by moving up and down all gears on the freewheel. If shifts to larger or smaller cogs are still a bit hesitant or noisy, tweak the barrel slightly clockwise or anticlockwise a quarter of a turn at a time, until the problem disappears.

cable adjusting barrel

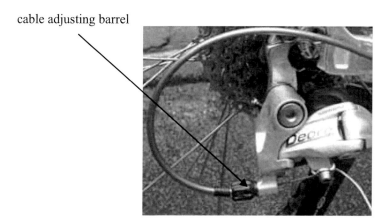

Photo 5

Chain Repair

The derailleur system, by its very design, does no favours whatsoever to the lifespan of the chain. As cage plates and pulleys twist and turn, repeated stress is placed on the moving parts of every single link and it's a minor miracle that this vital element of the drivetrain actually lasts as long as it does. Added to this (like the domestic hoover and the washing machine), the chain is the one component that is invariably neglected where maintenance is concerned. Dust, dirt and grime together with constant assault from the elements all take their toll, as does the occasional poor gear shifting technique of the cyclist. Wear and damage can be reduced considerably by adopting basic common sense measures such as easing pedal pressure when changing gear and avoiding the use of maximum crossover gear ratios; i.e. large chainring / large rear cog and small chainring / small rear cog - these extreme combinations create undue lateral strain. As a matter of regular maintenance of the chain and certainly after every long journey, excess dirt build-up should be cleaned off using a neutral detergent (not alkali based). It should then be lubricated, preferably with a wax lube such as 'White Lightening Clean

Ride'. These simple precautions will prolong its life and will help the efficient operation of the drivetrain in general.

However, when a chain does become badly worn (rusted or stretched), it must be replaced and this will probably mean a new rear freewheel cassette as well. Economising by replacing just the chain is a definite false economy, as it will only end up slipping badly on the back cogs, causing further damage. The front chainset, on the other hand, can usually be retained, but it's a good idea to have it checked out for wear at the same time.

If a chain link breaks, it can be repaired, providing you have spare links and the correct chain tool. The best is the screw type chain breaker - compact and easy to use but, note when doing so, that the key word is 'subtlety'. Note also, that there are two types of chain, depending on whether your rear freewheel has 6/7/8 cogs (narrow CN-HG50) or 9 cogs (super narrow CN-HG93).

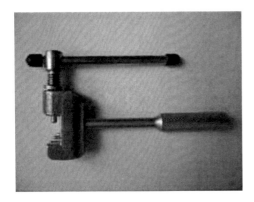

Chain Breaker

Fixing a broken segment of chain involves using the chain breaker to gently push the pin out of the link almost as far as it will go - but not completely (see photo 1). The broken link should then fall out. Inserting the new segment requires the removal of two links from the chain (male and female) and replacing them with two new ones. Once this is done, rejoin the chain by hand, having firstly turned it round so that the pin is facing you for easier access. Now place the chain in the chain breaker

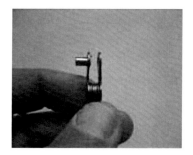

Photo 1

Photo 2

again (see photo 2) and wind the pin carefully back through the link plate. Check that it is raised the same distance above the rejoined plate as nearby pins in the chain. Finally, turn the crank slowly by hand to make sure the chain is running smoothly on all gears.

Brakes

Unless you go down the road of investing in an expensive hydraulic disc brake system, the best option for a touring bike is the cantilever V-brake. Easy to maintain and repair, the V-brake gives efficient stopping when carrying heavy loads and is far less problematic.

Initial set up should leave the brake blocks correctly lined up and flush with the rims and positioned no more than 1-2mm away - i.e. with a gap of 1-2mm between block surface and rim. The first point of adjustment is made at the brake lever by turning the cable adjusting barrel to decrease the gap and, at the same time, alter the amount of travel in the brake lever itself. Should the brake blocks not be contacting the rim simultaneously, the tension can be adjusted by unscrewing the cable anchor bolt on the V-brake (see page 26), testing as you go.

The other major setting, especially if there's excessive squealing from the brakes, is 'toe-in'. This ensures that the leading edge of the block makes contact with the rim first, giving quieter and more efficient braking. To accomplish this, loosen the brake block mounting bolts (see page 26) and move the blocks to the position shown in diagram 1, when viewed from above. Obviously, once the brakes are fully applied, the entire surface area of the block will then be in contact with the rim.

After any adjustment, always test the brakes by depressing the brake levers a few times and then rechecking alignment and clearance. The only remaining maintenance necessary is to make sure the brake block surfaces are clean and free from grit and to add the occasional drop of oil to moving parts.

Note that all brake blocks are provided with 'wear indicator' grooves (see diagram 2) and blocks should be replaced in pairs when these disappear down to a flat surface.

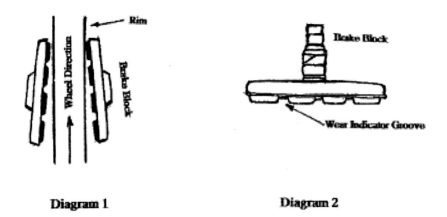

Diagram 1   Diagram 2

Wheels

Wheel maintenance is largely a matter of inspection. Check that the wheels are placed firmly in the 'drop-outs' and that quick release levers (standard on most decent tourers and hybrids) are secure. Check the rims for excessive scoring and that they haven't worn thin over time. Finally, make sure spokes aren't loose or broken and test the wheel to see if it's 'true' (i.e. not buckled). This can be done by slowly spinning the wheel and, using the gap between brake blocks and rim as a guide, seeing if the gap varies as the wheel revolves. Any minor variation, especially if all spokes are tight, is acceptable. Anything more than this, usually caused by uneven stress in the spokes, must be corrected. A spoke can be tightened or loosened by using a universal spoke key. Once you've found the 'slot' on the spoke key that fits the nipple on your particular wheel, turn clockwise to tighten and anticlockwise to slacken tension. Truing a wheel in this way, however, is a bit of an art-form and something that needs practice and, perhaps, a little advice from the friendly man at your local bike shop.

Spoke Key

If a spoke is actually broken and you're carrying spares, it's relatively easy to replace providing it's either on the front wheel or the left-hand side (opposite the gear side) of the rear wheel. In these cases, simply copy the way the broken spoke is threaded between rim and hub, making sure it's tight once fitted. If the broken spoke is attached to the hub at the derailleur gear side of the rear wheel, it inevitably means removing the freewheel cassette and this might be best done at the bike shop.

Whatever the problem, whether it's spoke replacement or a simple puncture, your initial job is to take the wheel off. For either wheel, first release the brake. If your bike has V-brakes, hold tightly together and then slip the cable out. Once the brake is loose and the quick release lever opened, the front wheel will just need a gentle tap down with the hand for it to drop out of the forks. When taking the rear wheel off, it's a good idea to shift the chain onto the smallest rear cog, which will make getting the wheel back on afterwards much easier. Pushing the rear wheel forward and downward will then bring the derailleur back and allow the wheel to drop out of the frame.

When it comes to reinstalling either front or rear wheel, ensure that it is central to the frame and don't forget to re-attach the brake cable. The quick release lever should be positioned on the left-hand side of the bike (as you sit), with the front lever closed behind the fork and the rear lever fixed between seat stay and chain stay. Always turn the adjusting nut (opposite end of the hub) until it is almost 'finger-tight' before locking off the quick release lever.

Fixing a Puncture

Running on good quality trekking tyres with inner Kevlar protection that are pumped up to the correct pressure will undoubtedly give you a better chance of mile after mile of trouble-free cycling. That said, as with death itself, punctures are inevitable. Reasons are many - the afore-mentioned low tyre pressure, road debris, misaligned rim strip, badly worn tyre, etc. Fortunately, fixing a puncture is easy and certainly when touring, this is made even easier by carrying a couple of spare inner tubes. That way, the problem can be quickly resolved on the road, with the punctured inner tube being fixed when you have more time. Apart from the spare inner tube, you'll also need two tyre levers and a puncture repair kit (see photos 1 and 2).

Photo 1   Photo 2

When the dreaded event does take place, the first thing to do is take off any panniers and bags and stand the bike upside down. Then undo the brake quick-release mechanism by 'pinching' the arms together and slipping the cable out. Whichever wheel is involved, loosen the quick-release lever on the hub and take the wheel off. If it's the rear wheel, shift your rear derailleur to the smallest cog to ease getting the wheel back on afterwards. Once off, unscrew the valve cap and the valve retaining nut at the base.

Next, deflate the tyre completely and ensure the tyre and tube are reasonably free on the rim. To get one side of the tyre off, place a tyre lever between tyre and rim and, bending it back, hook it on to a spoke. Using the second lever, perform the same trick a few inches further on (see photo 3). Repeat this until you're able to get one side completely free by hand. You can now push the valve up into the tyre and take out the punctured tube (see photo 4). Running your fingers inside and around the tyre, check for any thorns or bits of debris still embedded in the tyre; feel also for anything on the inner rim that could have caused the puncture.

Photo 3   Photo 4

Having slightly inflated the new inner tube to regain its shape, fit it back under the tyre and on to the rim, making sure the valve is sitting straight with the retaining nut secured. Starting at the valve end, now place the tyre back on to the rim. It should feed back easily enough at first, but you will probably need the tyre levers to push in the final few inches of sidewall (see photo 5). Be careful not to 'pinch' the inner tube at this stage.

Photo 5

Lastly, pump up the tyre to the correct pressure and replace it in the frame. Reconnect the brakes and turn the bike the right way up before 'centring' the wheel in the forks/frame. Tighten the adjusting nut on the hub and lock the quick-release lever in the correct position.

Your puncture repair kit should have patches, glue, chalk and sandpaper. Fixing the punctured inner tube means firstly finding the puncture. Inflate the tube and, holding it close to your ear, listen for the tell-tale hiss before marking its position with the chalk. If it's not immediately evident, pass the inflated tube through a bowl of water to locate the puncture.

Next, deflate the tube, roughen the area surrounding the hole with the sandpaper and spread some glue (big enough for a patch); leave it for a couple of minutes to become touch-dry. Peel the backing off a suitable patch and press it firmly down over the glued area, holding it for a minute or so. Any 'tackiness' around the patch can be dried off by dusting it with the chalk and sandpaper.

Leave the tube to set for about 15 minutes and partially inflate to check that the patch has taken. It can then be deflated and rolled up in readiness for your next inevitable puncture.

Bike Service

If you buy your bike from the local cycle shop, you should get a free initial service as part of the deal. This usually takes place after a set number of miles or a set time (3-6 months) when all the bits and pieces have fully 'bedded in'. In those first months of the life of your new bike, cables tend to stretch, nuts and bolts loosen and every other conceivable part that might need adjustment will do. As most decent cycle stores are members of the Association of Cycle Traders, the people who run them should have CyTech qualifications. This means that you're dealing with mechanics who will be able to solve all your problems, help answer all your questions and treat your prized possession with due reverence.

After the initial service, your bike should be checked out and serviced at least once a year and, regardless, before any longer trip you're contemplating. Many of the basic checks and much of the maintenance can, of course, be carried out by yourself. Brakes, lights, tyres (including pressures), gear adjustment, saddle height and level, etc. have already been dealt with. Other obvious maintenance issues such as lubrication of parts, cleaning and testing that all nuts and bolts are tight, can, again be done by the competent amateur. But, no matter how fastidious you are, the professional service can often identify problems that you wouldn't and will help answer specific queries before heading off on your expedition. The professional mechanic will also make a far better fist of tasks such as truing wheels or crank adjustments, which are not jobs easily mastered by the DIY cyclist and may need specialist tools.

Lastly, don't forget the hidden advantages of using your local cycle shop for regular servicing. They get to know your bike and its particular idiosyncrasies and you'll no doubt get favourable deals on parts, accessories and even your next new machine.

7

Body Maintenance - Health and Safety

The biggest myth in training for any sport is that 'there's no gain without pain'. This is especially true for cycle touring, so simply put in the miles, carb up and take it easy.

Gyms are awash with faces staring into the distance, toned torsos straining under weight and biceps bursting blood vessels. Rugby players will tell you that they've not been in a game unless flesh is bruised and bones are broken. I've seen marathon runners hitting the infamous 'wall' after pushing themselves too hard - god knows why, when just completing the 26 miles is demanding enough in itself. Even mountain biking and road racing can be designed to inflict untold misery on the human form if it's felt absolutely vital to test the body to its limits.

Thankfully, although building up your fitness for long-distance cycling is important, this can be tempered with common sense as no-one has yet invented a more efficient way of getting from A to B at a steady pace than riding a bike. It uses far less energy than walking or running and it's virtually impossible to pull muscles or damage joints due to the fact that the saddle, handlebars and pedals are fixed points. So, providing you use those fixed points sensibly and take reasonable steps as far as fitness and nutrition are concerned, little should go wrong.

Fitness

Cycle touring at home or abroad is well within the scope of anyone with a moderate degree of cycling fitness. There are obviously many other variables involved - length of tour, climate, terrain, daily mileage, etc. and, undoubtedly, the fitter you are, the better you will cope and the more you'll enjoy the experience. To make the most of it then, you'll need to put in some time before your trip and 'little and often' is the key - regular riding will open up all those tiny blood vessels that carry the oxygen and sugar more easily.

Taking part in other sports will undoubtedly improve your overall fitness but, like anything else, cycling fitness is activity specific. There is also a vast difference between touring and other forms of cycling. Exercising for a road race, where competitors can complete 100 to 200 miles in quick time is extremely intensive and demands peak physical fitness. This is the domain of the heart-rate monitor, anaerobic warm-ups and basal metabolic rates - issues that need not bother the average touring cyclist. Mountain bikers, again, require a totally different type of fitness, which involves upper-body strength and being able to manage the knocks and tumbles inherent in the sport. But for us 'bears of very little brain', there's no point worrying about your lactate threshold or hitting that 'wall'. When preparing for a tour, the slow and sensible option is best.

If you only have a limited cycling background, then you'll have to get general miles into your legs before embarking on a slightly more rigorous training regime. Easy rides at first, to get used to comfort, gearing and cadence (rate of pedalling). Then, after a basic training schedule (which is detailed below), aim at doing an initial 'serious' ride of around 25 miles - this is a good psychological watershed from which you can take on longer distances. Remember that reasonable cycling fitness only comes from practising at least three times a week over varying distances.

The schedule itself is aimed at the novice who intends completing a two week trip, averaging around 50 miles a day (including rest days). Please don't treat it as anything other than a guide and don't see it as a daunting task. I know many cyclists who do absolutely nothing before a tour, insisting that their fitness comes on the trip itself. Others believe in a belt and braces approach, spending hours in the gym and on the road before taking on any serious journey. Ultimately, it's down to you - what you feel best suites your own body and mind and how it can be tailored to fit your own specific needs.

This training schedule should begin three months or so before a 'longish' tour and shows the number of miles to be put in each day and week. It can then be followed by extended rides in the final four weeks.

Week	M	T	W	Th	F	S	Su
1	5	-	5	-	-	10	10
2	-	10	-	10	-	10	-
3	10	-	10	-	10	-	15
4	-	10	-	15	-	-	15
5	-	10	-	15	-	15	-
6	15	-	15	-	15	-	15
7	-	20	-	15	-	20	-
8	20	-	15	-	20	-	20

Don't worry if you can't keep to this exactly or, for whatever reason, you miss sessions but, at the end of it, you should feel more than capable of increasing the distance to your first 25 miler. After this, it's all in the mind and only occasionally in the backside. 30 miles, 40 miles and 50 miles are doable and, once you've turned that particular corner, you can consider yourself a 'fully-grown' touring cyclist.

Lastly, as you approach the big day, make sure you complete at least one 40 or 50 mile ride with full kit - i.e. with your bike hooked up to panniers loaded with 20 Kg. This not only gives you a more realistic picture of the forthcoming tour, but also irons out any problems you might have with the bike and how it handles under weight.

Nutrition

The body will cope without food for long periods, calling on reserves of fat and other forms of stored fuel long before it gives up on you. Without water though, you'll be in trouble fairly quickly. So, for cycling, hydration is just as important as nutrition. Even on cold days, you'll sweat (maybe imperceptibly) and this has to be replaced by appropriate liquids. Coffee, alcohol and fizzy drinks are not the answer. Water, fruit juice and sports drinks, which contain electrolyte replacement and other supplements, are the best way to rehydrate the system. If you're cycling through hot countries, you may need up to a litre an hour, dependent on humidity and terrain. Carry two full water bottles on your bike, with maybe a half-litre bottle in your pannier as reserve. Remember also, that empty water bottles develop moulds quite quickly, so clean them regularly.

On the nutrition front, if you really enjoy your food, as I do, then cycle touring is the perfect sport. If you're carrying 20 Kg and averaging 50 or 60 miles a day, you'll need around 5000 calories compared with the usual daily needs (for an active male) of 3000. Fuel up on large amounts of carbohydrates for energy, some protein for tissue and muscle maintenance and a little fat for long-term energy. Go for less-refined (complex, 'slow-release') carbohydrates such as pasta, rice, potatoes, bread, fruit (especially bananas) and vegetables. Protein in the form of chicken, fish, beans and eggs are best and always carry a supply of energy bars, biscuits, fruit, cheese, etc. in case you hit long stretches between eateries. Having said this, don't be too hard on yourself as far as diet is concerned. I certainly enjoy local dishes when abroad (that's half the fun) and I never feel guilty about downing a couple of beers at the end of a long, hard day in the saddle.

Ailments

Aches, pains, coughs and colds, although they should be taken seriously, hardly fall into the 'trip-busting' category of ailments. With most minor problems, simply give them a little time. If you're mid-tour, then reduce the pressure on that aching knee by wearing a support bandage, carry paracetamol to control a high temperature and use anti-inflammatories for swollen joints. If at all possible, take a rest day to speed up the healing process or at least re-adjust your schedule until you're feeling better. And, it's no good complaining to others because, chances are, there'll be nobody there to complain to. In any case, it's common knowledge that talking about your illness leaves 80 per cent of people bored, with the other 20 per cent secretly hoping that it gets worse.

Staying healthy and steering clear of avoidable ailments is largely a matter of common sense. When you're actually on the road, it's important to maintain a reasonable level of physical fitness and to take simple steps to guard against any minor health problems. Along with your overall cycling fitness, you'll need to exercise those parts of the body that will be called upon most i.e. upper and lower legs, arms and shoulders. For both endurance and flexibility, the muscles involved should be worked by following a program of stretches and strengtheners, which can be carried out as a simple 10 minute warm-up in your hotel room. Calf, hamstring, neck and lower back can be kept flexible by stretching. Arm, shoulder, thigh and stomach muscles can be toned using press-ups, sit-ups and crunches. Using such a routine will also help reduce common muscle and joint problems such as knee, neck, shoulder and back pain, although having said that, these are more often due to bad riding technique. The usual cause of knee pain is the use of too high a gear, especially on inclines, while shoulder, hand, neck and back complaints are often the result of incorrectly adjusted saddle and handlebars (see Size and Fit on page 46).

Assuming your fitness and bike 'set-up' have been taken care of, the only other factors that can ruin a perfect cycling holiday are basic health problems and minor illnesses. These have been listed below in no particular order or degree of importance.

Dehydration: Caused by excessive fluid loss either through sweating or illness (particularly diarrhoea), its symptoms are headache, dizziness and passing very concentrated urine. In extreme cases, dehydration can be dangerous and even fatal. Use the colour and quantity of your urine as a guide. You should be passing reasonable amounts of straw coloured urine but, if it darkens and the amount reduces, your fluid intake needs to be increased. Supplement this by mixing a rehydration sachet in water, which will help to replace lost minerals and salts.

Nutrition deficiency: Bearing in mind the number of calories required to sustain a long day in the saddle, this can occur if your diet is poor or insufficient. Sometimes referred to as 'the bonk' (an unfortunate American term), this is when your body runs out of fuel causing lethargy and weakness. When it happens, it must be addressed quickly by taking the obvious steps, but it is far better to avoid it completely by eating little and often throughout the day and managing a sensible diet throughout your tour.

Sores and blisters: Saddle sores are either the product of an incorrect or poorly adjusted saddle (see page 29) or simply a case of riding long distances in warm conditions. This particular problem can be minimized by wearing clean, padded bike shorts and showering properly at the end of each day. Using moisturising cream or nappy-rash cream before setting off also helps.

Hands are best protected by wearing padded, fingerless gloves to reduce numbness and blisters, whilst using cycling shoes or stiff-soled shoes will protect your feet. Avoid running shoes/trainers, which are specially designed to absorb impact and, therefore, compress on each pedal stroke. This will result in wasting some of the energy every time you push down instead of transferring all that power directly to the pedal, and so makes for very inefficient cycling.

Toothache: Nagging toothache can ruin your trip and, if neglected, can easily lead to a gum abscess or, worse still, an infection. Before any long journey, especially if it's abroad, have a dental check-up and do it well in advance. This will allow any treatment to settle prior to travelling.

Diarrhoea: Change of climate and food, as well as cross-contamination, can cause diarrhoea. It is debilitating at best and, like toothache, will seriously affect any cycling trip. If it strikes, make sure you replace fluids - plenty of water supplemented with a rehydration solution is the usual treatment. Avoid rich foods by keeping to a very bland diet such as grilled chicken breast and boiled potatoes. No alcohol, no coffee, no fizzy drinks - stick to weak tea with a little sugar.

Heat exhaustion / Heatstroke: Normally the result of excessive dehydration, where the body's heat regulation system breaks down. Heat exhaustion soon follows with its associated symptoms of severe headaches, muscle cramps and fatigue. At this stage, the only remedy is to rest and increase your fluid intake (but gradually). Salt tablets may also help.

In extreme cases, after prolonged periods of exposure to high temperatures, heatstroke can occur. Sweating diminishes and, to compensate, blood rushes from the brain in an attempt to cool the body down. Symptoms are sickness, high body temperature and lack of co-ordination and, if not dealt with (preferably in hospital), it will quickly cause unconsciousness. If recognised in time, cool off under a wet sheet and drink lots of water.

Bites and stings: Even in northern European countries, mosquitoes are a problem. Avoid by wearing long sleeves, socks and trousers in the evening (mosquitoes are especially attracted to the smell of feet) and by using mosquito repellent. Try to take rooms with air conditioning to save leaving windows open at night.

Bee and wasp stings are only an issue if you have an allergy, in which case, medical help should be sought. Otherwise, calamine lotion will ease the discomfort.

Some countries produce their own particular nightmares in the 'insect department' - ants, spiders, even scorpions can be commonplace and should be steered well clear of. Tempting as it is to take your shoes off while resting, it's not a good idea and always shake out shoes and clothing before getting dressed in the morning.

Cuts and grazes: Clean minor cuts and scrapes with antiseptic wipes and cover with a light dressing if necessary. If bleeding doesn't stop within 15 minutes of applying direct pressure, a cut may need a stitch or two. Change any dressing daily and keep the wound clean whilst healing, but seek medical advice if it becomes infected.

Sunburn: This is not a matter of gradually developing a healthy tan, more a case of excessive exposure to the sun. Don't let it happen - wear appropriate light clothing covering shoulders especially, avoid cycling during the hottest part of the day and use plenty of sunscreen and/or sun block.

Vaccinations: Again, this will depend on where you are touring, but it's always advisable to at least keep your tetanus jabs up to date. Your local clinic/GP will tell you what you need in terms of vaccinations before any foreign trip.

Finally, make sure you take a standard first-aid kit with you. There are a number of kits on the market that are specifically aimed at the cyclist and you can add your own bits and pieces to cover other eventualities. Always re-check the contents before a trip and replace any expired items. I've itemized some basics below but, obviously, this is a flexible list which can vary according to the part of the world you're cycling in.

Plasters (various sizes)	Antiseptic wipes
Sterile dressings	Thermometer
Adhesive dressings	Calamine lotion
Gauze pads	Mosquito repellent
Bandages (including elasticated)	Syringes and needles
Scissors	Paracetamol / Ibuprofen
Safety pins	Sunscreen
Disposable gloves	Rehydration sachets
Salt tablets	Tweezers

Safe Cycling

Having dealt with how to keep the body in shape for cycling, we can now
turn to the more obvious points of cycling safely, which will hopefully
limit the chances of things going wrong whilst on your bike. It would be
impossible to cater for every contingency. Being chased by a stray dog,
dealing with road rage, injuries sustained in collisions, etc. have to be met
and resolved as and when they occur, but there's a wealth of sound
guidance on the more mundane safety issues to be found in the pages of
the Highway Code.

- Use cycle paths wherever possible.
- Cycle in single-file on narrow or busy roads.
- At roundabouts, keep to the left or dismount and walk around.
- Use bus-lanes only if signs say that you can.
- Don't cycle on pavements unless segregated cycle-lanes are
  painted on.
- Do not ride under the influence of alcohol or drugs (police can't
  demand a breath-test, but will test you on the old 'walk in a
  straight line' principle).
- At night, you must have front and rear lights lit, plus a red rear
  reflector and amber pedal reflectors.

Obviously, most of this advice applies to urban/city cycling in traffic,
but this, after all, is where your health is most at risk. Supermodel, Elle
('the body') Macpherson, was recently caught on camera riding her bike
minus helmet and with her 5 year-old son sat on the handlebars. As she
weaved through the city streets of London, she apparently had a definite
'no comment' look on her face - hardly a great model of the 'role'
variety! Other no-no's include ignoring red traffic lights when turning left
(many cyclists do) and riding along roads at 20 miles an hour with your
dog in tow.

For the touring cyclist, a major safety issue is getting used to handling a
fully laden bike. Learn to approach bends with care (i.e. slowly) and
don't lean into corners as hard as you normally would. When descending

long hills, slow your loaded machine by 'feathering' the brakes so that rims don't overheat (which can cause a blow-out). Don't hug the kerb, where the road is usually rutted and interrupted by drains - try to ride a couple of feet in from the edge of the pavement. Along rougher tarmac, take your weight slightly off the saddle, allowing your legs to absorb the shock. Always scan well ahead for any potential problems, especially cars coming out of side-roads and hazards such as large potholes or road works. And, remember that, for all cyclists, it's most dangerous in moderately busy road conditions, where you're tempted to go faster or weave through the traffic - when it's more congested, it's paradoxically safer.

All that said, life itself is a risk and, compared with cycling, only golf and rambling are safer. Fishing, for instance, is over 40 times as dangerous as far as fatalities are concerned.

Safety Abroad

Many of the issues regarding health and safety whilst touring overseas have already been touched upon earlier in this chapter. For northern European countries (and other temperate areas of the world), what applies here also applies there. Local environmental hazards, however, could have an impact - if you're brave enough to traverse the Alps or the High Tatras mountains, altitude sickness may be a problem and, in some parts of Eastern Europe, rabies and insect-borne diseases are still commonplace. As with all foreign travel, check with your GP as to which vaccinations you will need before setting off and be aware of the risks of sexually transmitted diseases, such as hepatitis B and HIV, no matter where your cycle tour takes you.

   If your ambitions involve, say, a journey to the Middle East, your immunisation plan might include malaria medication and vaccinations for diphtheria/tetanus, polio and typhoid. Your medical kit should also contain antibiotics, antifungal cream and water-purification tablets (if you're cycling in more remote areas) and, in any case, the golden rule here is to always use bottled water and avoid ice in drinks.

Wherever you find yourself, make sure you have adequate travel insurance. Even in Europe, back up your E111 with an insurance policy that will cover other eventualities including loss of passport, theft, etc. Check the small print, especially on options for lower medical expenses as, for example, the USA have extremely high medical costs.

Look out for exclusions, such as some sporting activities and even certain countries. And it's also a good idea to make a photocopy of all your travel documents - passport, visas, insurance certificates, air-tickets, etc., and keep this in a safe place (not in the same bag as your originals).

Once across the water, if you're travelling independently, health and safety is firmly in your own hands. Take account of the country's climatic conditions and plan your route accordingly, incorporating rest days where you can. Be aware of the differences you'll face, especially the obvious ones like cycling on the right-hand side of the road. Many European (and other) destinations insist that cyclists use designated cycle paths both in urban and more rural areas. Follow the rules of the road wherever you are and, also, use your common sense regarding personal security. Don't leave your bike unattended and unlocked and don't leave bags out of sight.

As for accommodation, if you are not using a tent, there are over 4000 youth hostels to be found worldwide. Contact the YHA for a copy of their International Guide, which gives complete details of many of them, as well as other information on visas, time zones and currency. For hotels and guesthouses, it's useful to carry a copy of the local Rough Guide or Lonely Planet book. Internet cafes now make booking ahead relatively easy but, personally, I've had few problems finding accommodation 'on the hoof', no matter where in the world I've travelled. Usually, it's simply a case of visiting a tourist information office or asking in a bar/café if they know where a room can be had. And finally, although English has now become the accepted international language, it is still helpful if you've at least a basic grasp of a country's mother tongue when looking for somewhere to stay.

8

Loading Your Bike - Balancing Bags

Never carry anything more on your shoulders than a passionate desire
to travel - instead, let the bike take the strain.

Packing for Tours

If you work on the premise that most touring involves either
day/weekend trips or longer expeditions, then loading your bike takes on
one of two basic arrangements. Shorter escapes can be done on two rear
panniers and a bar bag. This will undoubtedly give you more capacity
than you'll actually need, but it does mean that everything's reasonably
well-balanced and that frequently needed items are accessible. In any
case, valuables such as money, camera, documents, etc. are probably
safer in a bar bag, as it can be quickly detached and carried when calling
at shops, cafes and other 'stop-offs'.

   Obviously, much more thought has to be put into extended cycle
journeys. Turning days into weeks demands more equipment, clothing
and spares in order to cover the variations in terrain and weather. Having
said that, don't let the idea of carrying all that gear put you off. On the
flat, once you've built your speed up, the bike's momentum will help you
along. And when you hit those hills, a sensible use of the lower gears will
ease the added effort needed to get you to the top. To cope with that extra
weight (i.e. 15 Kg plus), the best configuration for a touring bike is two
low-mounted front panniers together with the rear panniers, a tool bag
and a bar bag (see page 90). Balancing that load has to be carefully
considered - around 60 per cent of the weight at the back and 40 per cent
at the front. To further improve road handling, heavy items should always
be packed low down in your front panniers, with attention paid to
distributing the weight evenly on both sides. Again, for rear panniers

make sure you have roughly equal loads either side and place the panniers as centrally as possible over the rear hub.

Other common-sense measures are as follows:-

1. Regardless of whether or not your kit is waterproof, it's a good idea to put everything in separate plastic bags. Heavy rainfall and deep puddles seem to have a nasty habit of somehow forcing water in and the other side of the coin dictates that anything that can spill or leak will do. This belt and braces approach of putting everything in plastic bags before packing your panniers might appear a little over the top, but the day you don't do it is the day you wish you had. It also helps if the bags are transparent, making for easier identification of contents.

2. Avoid buying panniers with too many side pockets - one is sufficient. Apart from confusing yourself on what they all contain, they tend to provide added temptation to the opportunist thief. Also, more pockets mean more seams, which in turn, lead to an increased risk of leaks.

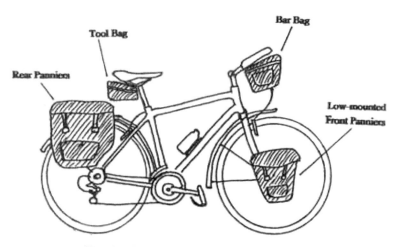

Pannier Configuration for Touring

3. When packing your panniers, do it in a methodical and organised way, making it easier to locate your separate bags containing clothes, spares, first-aid kit, etc. Compartmentalising and getting to know what's in each pannier during your tour eliminates having to empty them all to find your chewing gum. You can even use colour-coded bags for the panniers so that you load consistently by packing things in the same place each time. Always have a little spare space in one of your panniers for anything you buy on the road, such as snacks and drinks.

4. Don't overload your bar bag. Remember, it's there for valuables and essentials such as sunglasses, maps, camera, guide books, etc. Ensure, also, that rear panniers are positioned to give enough heel clearance when cycling.

5. Make occasional checks, especially on long trips, on both rack and pannier attachments. Look for wear on mounting clips and rack tubing and ensure all bolts are tight. Using electrical tape on pannier to rack contact points can reduce any play and protect tubing. It's also a good idea to give your fully loaded bike a trial run before setting off on a tour. See how well it performs on hills and rough tracks and adjust panniers and what they contain accordingly. Bear in mind that the bike's breaking system is only designed to arrest an unladen machine - so 'retrain' yourself in managing downhills and emergency stops.

6. For those who prefer camping to hostels or B&B's, use a bungee strap to attach any bulky but light items on the rear rack. These would include tent, sleeping mat and sleeping bag and can be placed between your panniers in waterproof bags. Even if you don't intend to camp, the bungee is still handy for holding waterproofs on those days when the weather is 'on-off'.

7. Carry spare mounting clips, nuts and bolts for the racks and a good needle and strong thread with you on a long journey. An ability to DIY 'mend and make do' on the road is invaluable, especially if you're travelling through foreign parts.

Travelling by Ferry

There's not a lot to say about 'packing' your bike when heading across the water by ferry - the configuration of panniers and bags will be much the same as that adopted for tours at home. It's more a case of deciding what you want to unpack for the time you'll be spending on board as, once your bike is securely locked on the car deck, there's no going back until the ferry arrives at its destination. There is, however, quite a lot of useful advice and information to give regarding the actual 'travelling by ferry', so we might as well deal with that aspect in this particular chapter.

Our island is bordered by the North Sea, the Irish Sea and the English Channel and all crossings to mainland Europe, Scandinavia and Ireland are well served by various ferry companies. There is also a wide choice of ports around the country to help link your home town with your final destination. France and Spain can be reached from the south-coast ports, with the Channel Tunnel as a further option. If you live in the north of England, you can get to the Netherlands and Belgium from Hull or Newcastle. Similarly, Scandinavian destinations are routed from these two northern cities and several others along the west coast of Britain serve the east coast of Ireland. If you're not using your own transport to take you and your bike to these embarkation points, then you can book a rail ticket instead. Trains usually have separate compartments for transporting bikes and costs are nominal (sometimes free). Certainly, if you plan well ahead, train fares are relatively cheap and the journey provides a relaxing start to any foreign cycle tour without the worry of wondering where to park your car at the port. In the table on the next page, I've listed a sample of ferry crossings, but this is only a brief illustration and is not meant to be an up to date or comprehensive summary of routes.

As far as formalities are concerned, taking your bike across the water couldn't be easier. Simply sort out your ferry ticket by phone or online and, as long as you don't forget your passport, everything's fairly 'idiot-proof'. At the port, your ferry departure point will be well sign-posted and there are always plenty of harbour and ferry staff on duty to direct you to the correct queue. Usually, you'll be sent to the front of the long line of cars and caravans and straight up the metal ramp. Once on board, crew members will show you where you can leave your bike and baggage - normally, tied by an oily rope to a barrier in a dark corner of the car deck. Again, don't forget to take everything you need with you (especially if it's an overnight ferry), before heading for the lift to the main decks and make a mental note of which car deck your bike is on.

Route	Operator	Duration
France		
Dover-Calais	P&O	1hr 30min
Portsmouth-Caen	Brittany	5hr 45min
Plymouth-Roscoff	"	5hr 30min
Poole-Cherbourg	"	4hr 15min
Belgium		
Hull-Zeebrugge	P&O	12hr 45min
Netherlands		
Hull-Rotterdam	P&O	10hr 15min
Newcastle-Amsterdam	DFDS	15hr 30min
Spain		
Portsmouth-Bilbao	P&O	35hr
Plymouth-Santander	Brittany	25hr
Ireland		
Holyhead-Dublin	Stena	3hr 30min
Stranraer-Belfast	"	2hr 50min
Denmark		
Harwich-Esbjerg	DFDS	24hr 15min

These days, modern ferries have more than enough onboard facilities to keep you entertained, especially on the longer trips from the south coast to northern Spain. Ensuite cabins, cafes, restaurants, bars, cinemas, gyms, live music, casinos, shopping - the lot. Standards are generally very good and the crossing gives you chance to chill out and think through your first day's cycle for when you touch down on foreign soil. If this is your first cycling adventure abroad, it's definitely a stress-free way of getting you and your bike to the starting point.

Finally, when you eventually dock, you'll be called back down to the car deck and should have enough time to untie your bike, replace any panniers and bags and check that all is well. Sensibly, most ferries allow you a head start down the ramp to escape the exhaust fumes as car engines are fired up. Then it's a cursory glance at passport control and customs before you're off into the sunshine, hopefully remembering that you'll now be cycling on the right-hand side of the road.

Packing for Air Travel

As far as actually buying your air ticket is concerned, a lot depends on the destination and the duration of your tour. Sources for obtaining tickets are many and varied. Charter flight bargains can be found via the Internet, through discount ticket agencies and 'bucket shops' or by using your local travel agent, but these will limit you to a standard one or two week trip. If you intend embarking on a longer cycle tour or heading for a more obscure destination, then you'll undoubtedly end up paying for the privilege. Look at the travel pages of the national Sunday papers or contact specialists such as Trailfinders or STA Travel and note, that as a general rule, cheaper tickets will have to be booked well in advance. Whatever you decide, it's a good idea to get a direct international flight, as changing mid-stream increases the risk of your bike and baggage ending up in Düsseldorf as you set foot in Damascus. Again, you may end up paying more.

Once you've done your research on the best available flight and, certainly before you purchase your ticket, ask about weight allowances and whether there's a separate charge for your bicycle. A few airlines will carry a bike free of charge - some don't even count its weight as part of your allowance. If this is not the case, then your 20 Kg (44 lbs) limit means that you must be extremely disciplined when you take the bike's 12 or 13 Kg weight into account. Pack as much as you dare into your hand luggage (usually 5 Kg) and hope that the rest doesn't tip you into 'excess baggage' payments. Also, bear in mind that the information you get over the phone may not reflect the airline's official policy on baggage. Sometimes it depends on just who you're talking to and so it's a good idea to have any concessions regarding your bike added to the passenger file. Often, getting to the airport check-in desk early and being friendly, patient and polite will go a long way with the check-in staff if you're a few pounds overweight.

Having got your plane ticket, make sure you carefully follow the airline's instructions on how to present your bike for transportation. Some companies only require the basics of turning handlebars through 90 degrees, removing pedals and deflating tyres. My advice is 'do this at your peril' - trusting baggage handlers to be gentle with your prized possession is about as sensible as putting vampires in charge of a blood bank. Nothing could be worse at the start of your foreign tour, than scooping your bike off the airport carousel with shattered mudguards, broken spokes and a torn saddle. The simple answer is the bike box, which your friendly local cycle shop will be more than happy to supply you with. These are the cardboard boxes that all new bikes are delivered in and come in various sizes. If possible, go for the largest, but first check your air ticket regarding any limitations on its length, width and height. An alternative to the free cardboard box is a purpose-specific bike bag such as the Evoc Bike Travel Bag, obviously a far better (although more expensive) solution that can be used on every trip. Much depends on what you do when you arrive at your destination and, if indeed, you'll be travelling back by air or by ferry. Some hotels will store your travel bag or cardboard box for when you return, but if it's a one-way air ticket you can discard the box at the airport.

Whatever you choose, the following pointers should help you to pack your bike so that it will be secure in its box and relatively easy to reassemble when you get there.

1. Remove both pedals and re-insert them in the cranks so that they're now facing inwards. To avoid scratching the down tube, it's a good idea to tape some cardboard round each pedal. Note also, that the pedal axles are marked 'R' and 'L' showing which is right and which is left.

2. Loosen the handlebar stem bolt and turn the bars through 90 degrees, so that they're in line with the frame. Make sure that you mark the height of the stem with a felt-tip pen before you drop it in the head tube.

3. Remove the saddle and seatpost, so that they can later be stored in the box. Again, mark the seatpost height before removing it.

4. Partially deflate both tyres (to account for the increase in air pressure) and take off the front wheel. This can then be placed beside the frame on the opposite side to the chainset.

5. If your box is large enough, you should now be able to put the frame with rear wheel and rear pannier racks still attached into the box, so that it's resting on the front forks and chainset. Cover and tape any sharp items (such as the chainset) with cardboard first and wrap a rag around the chain and rear sprockets. If necessary, take off the front pannier racks and place them beside the frame opposite the front wheel.

6. Put the saddle, tool bag and one of the front panniers in a vacant space in the box, making sure that you've secured all parts as best as possible. The other front pannier can be taken as hand luggage and the two rear panniers can be taped together and loaded as baggage.

9

Touring - A Trilogy of Trips

If you're not living on the edge, then you're taking up too much space.

On Motivation

There have already been enough books written on cycle tours to fill a library - detailed and graphic descriptions of routes around Britain and further afield containing masses of information on terrain, accommodation, attractions, watering holes and how to get there and back. No stone is left unturned, regardless of it being a short, medium or long trip and all with a wide choice of off-road, country or urban adventures. London's Docklands, the famous Tissington Trail, Devon's Coast to Coast, Land's End to John O'Groats, even a circular route round Iceland - it's all been done. And if you can't find a book or magazine on a particular tour, then there's the usual tsunami of material to be had on the Internet.

This chapter is not about going over old ground. It's not about routes, distances and gradients, or the underlying practicalities of taking on a cycle tour. It's not even about planning or fitness or any other factors (most of which have already been dealt with) that are, nevertheless, central to a successful journey. The following pages are an attempt at encouraging the novice who's setting out on a sunny morning for a day's cycle. They're concerned with motivating the more experienced cyclist who's thinking of pushing the boundaries towards a weekend trip, maybe with the family or a group of friends. They are unashamedly aimed at evoking the adventurer in all of us - at planting the seed of doubt that to stay where it's safe isn't such a basic instinct after all; that we have a secret need to live life just a little more dangerously. An existence which runs laboriously along tram lines through some unending, carefully structured sanctuary surely can't be too healthy in any case. 'A life where nothing's gained and nothing's lost ….. at such a cost' - there's got to be more to it than this.

I'm not suggesting that touring by bike will put you on some permanent 'high' or give you a self-sustaining adrenalin rush. There are probably greater highs and lows to be had by watching your local football team on a Saturday afternoon. But certainly on longer journeys, there is a definite 'pit of the stomach' moment as you head off into the unknown - not being aware of what the next day will bring, what you might come across, who you might meet. A bit like your first date with someone new, no matter how many times you've done it before, you still feel that same excitement and get that same buzz when starting out.

So, the alternatives are two weeks on a beach somewhere or to travel, meet new people and see new places. Choosing the latter means you'll come back far more charged, far more fulfilled and feeling that you've actually done something with your life, if only for a short time. After a few trips, you become addicted. You put up with the bad times and feel really alive the rest of the time. You may get accused of being mad, brave, selfish and self-centred, and pointed at by normal people who say 'most normal people wouldn't do that' - possibly with some justification. Certainly, if you travel alone, you have got to be a little self-centred and you have to be happy with your own company, but the advantages tend to outweigh the disadvantages. There's no lowest common denominator to deal with in the planning or the execution when you're on your own. You don't have to negotiate with a travelling partner what you'll do that day, how far you'll cycle, when to rest, where to stay, when to eat, when to stop. All this is down to you. Is that brave or mad or selfish or, perhaps, all of these? It's undoubtedly a personal thing and becomes a case of just how scary you find the prospect of total self-reliance. In the end, it's for you to decide whether to go solo, with someone else or in a group.

As always, you need to walk before you can run. Day trips start from your own back door. Year round, rain or shine, they require minimal planning, a packed lunch and usually end up at a pub. Whether you live in town or in the country, you can always find destinations to make for and routes can be varied to suit conditions and the time of year. A few hours cycling on a crisp winter's morning can be just as rewarding as a long day in the saddle in summer - seasons colour your journey, but they make it no less enjoyable.

It's a natural progression, often through getting together with cycling friends, to then move on to weekend tours with an overnight stop. A deathly dull week in the office can be made almost bearable at the thought of a Saturday morning escape to the Lakes or Wales or wherever, armed with bike, maps and a purpose. Again, it's your choice what you take on - canal towpaths, disused railway lines, country lanes or a mixture. Having fixed your destination, you can use your overnight stop as the focal point or you can plan a circular route with the sleepover roughly half-way round. A booking at a hostel or hiring a camping barn sorts out the accommodation and then it's just a matter of enjoying yourself, the company and the scenery. You usually return exhausted but, at the same time, rejuvenated and with a sense of having made the very best of your valuable days off. How many weekends and bank holidays have been wasted by the human race in general, mowing lawns, decorating bedrooms or taking work home, when they could have been spent usefully in the fresh air and under wide open skies? 'I wish I would have worked a little harder' is not a good epitaph to have etched on your gravestone.

Longer journeys are something you can feed off for months. So exciting at the 'development' stage - organising your route, doing the research, asking all the questions and also having to acknowledge that the dreaded list will end up becoming your best friend. Nearer the time, emotions often swing between over-excitement (to the extent that everything else in life takes second place) to nagging doubts on whether you should even be contemplating such a venture. Reassurance comes with pragmatism. Servicing the bike, gathering the required accessories and making sure the panniers are balanced, soon have the desired effect of placing your feet firmly back on the ground. Getting your gear laid out on the bed, checking your list, packing, taking it apart and then repacking again, and all those demons disappear.

My own first 'long' cycle tour started in Manchester, where I boarded an Intercity for London (together with my bike) and then spent three weeks zig-zagging my way back home. Towns, villages, hostels, cheap B&B's, good food and drink and wonderful weather (not always guaranteed) and, as with anything you do for the first time, it was completely unforgettable. Going solo wasn't an issue. It's incredible how willing people are to chat to you when you're on your own. If you're a couple, they leave you alone. I met some amazing characters on that journey, one of whom became a life-long friend.

Next trip, I caught a ferry at Portsmouth with my girlfriend. We sailed to Santander in northern Spain and had a fantastic holiday cycling over the Pyrenees and up along the west coast of France, before catching a ferry back from Brittany.

Having decided that I'd definitely caught the adventure bug, the following year I flew to the Lebanon, getting some strange looks at Beirut Airport as I reassembled my bike by the carousel. It then took just over five weeks to cycle the 2300 miles back through Syria, Turkey, Greece, Italy, over the Alps to Switzerland and finally the long push north through Europe - as you might imagine, a very memorable journey.

More recently, I followed the course of three major rivers back home from Eastern Europe - the Danube (from Bulgaria to Austria), the Otrava (through the Czech Republic to Germany) and the River Elbe to Hamburg - some 2000 miles in total.

My only bike ride south of the Tropics was a circular around Cuba. A fascinating country, which was then still very much in the grip of Fidel Castro and coloured by 1950's American cars and the sound of Salsa everywhere you went. Certainly not the standard package to the island's beach resorts (where you could be anywhere in the world from Tenerife to Florida), but a true eye-opener into the country's culture and people.

Some of these journeys might seem a little ambitious. You do have to be organised and you do need determination. But that's all it takes. As for fitness, so long as you have a reasonable level, you get the rest of it on the trip. You tend to be able to cope with things that go wrong because you have to and, when things go right, it gives you all the lift and the stimulus you need. Build in 'rest days' - extra time in your itinerary - should it become necessary for whatever reason. Maybe you'll want another day to look at the sights or maybe there's an event nearby which takes you slightly off route. It might even be a morning taken up for a repair to your bike or a day's illness or atrocious weather or really poor roads. Many different causes could add to your schedule.

If it's a British or European tour you're considering, sort out a potential route covering all the places and sights you want to see. Know what daily mileage you're capable of - as a rough guide, this should be no more than two-thirds of the mileage you could do as a one-off. Play around with distances and destinations until everything just about fits and then take account of the time and the funding available. For hostels and cheap rooms, rather than camping, I'd normally set aside around £40 a day (accommodation, food, beer, etc.). Finally, go back to your route, add in rest days and if it doesn't mesh, see where any adjustments can be made.

Once you're actually under way, the one thing you quickly learn is to take it a day at a time. Expect little, but always hope for a little more. You may feel apprehensive initially. Have you got everything you need? Will the bike turn up at the airport? What if the weather's bad? What if your fitness lets you down? Things (unbelievably) usually work out fine and the rest is a case of positive thinking, self-reliance and putting any minor mishaps in perspective and behind you. You're out there to enjoy yourself, to experience something you may never get chance to again, so savour those days on the road and treasure those moments of discovery - you'll remember them forever.

Day Trips

Two-thirds of the population lives in built-up suburban or inner city areas. If you fall into this category, the main difficulty, as far as cycling is concerned, is finding enough variation in routes around your immediate locality. Some of us might be fortunate enough to have an urban cycleway or canal towpath nearby, which we can use to whisk us off to that world of green on our doorstep. But, for many day-tripping cyclists, it's a case of fighting your way along busy roads or using your own or public transport to get your bike onto a quieter patch.

So, unless you're happy cycling in traffic, to become really serious about getting away for the day, you'll have to organise an escape route that can be used time after time and one that gives you lots of options. This might be in the form of the local railway station, which you can use to transport you and your bike to wherever the rail track leads. Trains have become much more user-friendly in recent years and there's often a special carriage allocated for bikes. The added advantage of taking the train is that you can get off at one station and come back from another and, if you're clever, you can guarantee a tailwind all the way.

If you go by car, this advantage melts away, as where you start from obviously becomes the end of your day's cycle as well. There's also the usual problem of whether to fit a bike rack or stow your bike inside, which might mean dismantling it first. On the plus side, you're not nailed to a timetable and your range of destinations is far greater.

Whatever the problems encountered in breaking free of the suburban jungle, don't give up. Continue to be single-minded in your determination to enjoy a day trip on your bike and, if you're one of the fortunate third who can arrange wonderful rides from your back door, then thank your lucky stars.

Around Lancashire's Coastal Plain

There's something quintessentially English about a trip to an old-fashioned seaside resort and along Lancashire's coastline you're spoilt for choice. Just a few miles north of its more famous neighbour

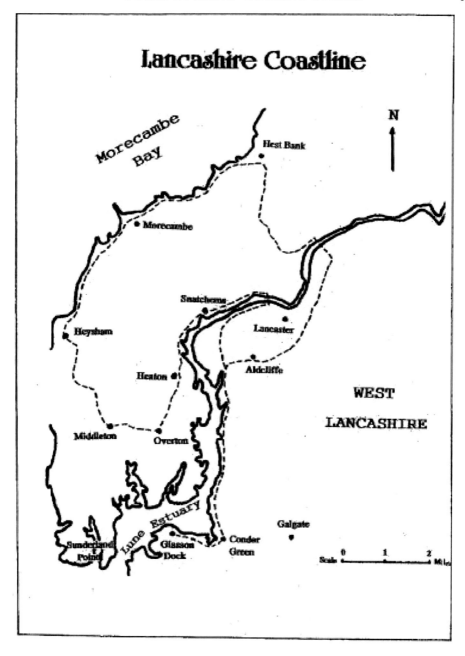

Lancashire Coastline

Blackpool, is the town of Morecambe - slightly down at heel in parts, but boasting uninterrupted views of the spectacular bay and the distant Lakeland peaks. Morecambe is a place that hasn't quite worked out its ultimate direction. In reality, this is bucket and spade country, fish and chips, bingo halls, amusement arcades and row upon row of B&B's - some good, some not so good. Although a pot of money has recently been spent by the local authority (much of it to good effect), visitors are still sadly lacking in the sorts of numbers that would make a marked difference to the local economy.

That's a shame because, without doubt, Morecambe is one of those destinations not to be missed. There's a new and superb promenade that seems to go on forever, an elegant stone jetty pushing out into the bay with the mountains of the southern Lakes feeling almost within reach and, nearby, a photo opportunity at Eric Morecambe's iconic statue. Meticulously manicured gardens with water fountains border the west end of the town's promenade and splendid Victorian terraces (some admittedly in need of a lick of paint) overlook large sections of the sea front.

But for me, the shining star of Morecambe is the 'Art Deco' Midland Hotel. Until a few years ago, it was boarded-up and derelict, tragically caught on the fly-paper of life, but following a marriage of private and public funding, this imposing crescent of 1930's opulence has now been lovingly restored to its former glory. A modernist masterpiece that was once a refuge for the rich and the famous, the Midland was the first hotel of its kind to be built on these shores. Inside, a stunning spiral staircase elegantly climbs its way past seahorse mosaics up to an ornate domed ceiling. There are rooftop suites, a sea view restaurant, a Rotunda bar, sun decks and a spa, all oozing style and seemingly frozen in time. From its chic café terrace with its 'must visit' loo, it looks out across the bay and, like some land-locked Queen Mary, commands prime position at the foot of the jetty.

Usually a day's cycle has one, or maybe two, genuine focal points - places of interest that form the heart of what you remember. Including Morecambe, this trip is blessed with four - all of them capable of standing on their own as destinations well worth visiting and all in stark contrast with each other.

The starting point is Glasson Dock, a fascinating 200 year old working port with a picturesque marina, locks, a swing bridge, two decent pubs and an excellent 'chippy'. Situated at the mouth of the Lune Estuary, Glasson lies directly opposite Sunderland Point, which in its colonial heyday was another thriving port, prospering on the back of the slave trade. A poignant reminder of those times can be found here in the form of Sambo's grave, serving as a rather grim and silent witness to a darker period in our history.

From Glasson Dock, it's an easy ride along the Lune Estuary Cycle Path - a mixture of gravel and tarmac hugging the waterline for the first few miles of the journey before turning off towards the village of Aldcliffe. Then, it's on to a section of the canal towpath into Lancaster, a city with over 2000 years of history, spanning everything from Roman excavations to Georgian architecture. South of the river, there's a castle, a cathedral, a Victorian folly set in landscaped parkland and an award-winning maritime museum at St George's Quay. In the city's bustling Market Square you'll find more impressive Victorian buildings, surrounded by narrow alleyways, cobbled streets, cosy pubs and cafes.

Finding your way back to the canal towpath, the route now winds north to the Lune Aquaduct with views over the river and the city skyline. Staying with the towpath and heading for the sea at Hest Bank, there's an opportunity to take time out to have a walk up the foreshore before turning on to the coastal road. From here, the promenade follows the coastline into Morecambe, where a welcome coffee break can be had on the terrace of the historic Midland Hotel. Another couple of miles relaxed cycling along the prom and you arrive at Heysham.

If Morecambe's spectacular seascape is the scenic attraction of this journey and Lancaster its cultural hook, then Heysham provides the tranquillity and charm of a picture postcard village set above an empty beach and with its own unique piece of history. Quaint old cottages line Main Street and take you down to St Patrick's church, behind which lies a strange collection of Viking stone 'coffins' overlooking the bay. The village's one and only pub serves real ale and home-cooked food in a friendly atmosphere and, if you don't fancy pub grub, there's an excellent café at the top of the street.

The road home involves cycling initially down quiet country lanes, via Middleton, Heaton with Oxcliffe and the even more oddly named settlement of Snatchems, probably associated historically with the naval pressgangs. A short stretch of cycle track then follows the banks of the Lune and brings you back to Lancaster and the Millennium Bridge. Once over the river, the Estuary Cycle Path returns you to Glasson Dock, the only part of the route that you revisit.

This 30 miles cycle could easily be extended to a two-day tour by making a circuit south of Glasson to Garstang, the heritage village of Dolphinholme and back via Galgate. Using the Stork Inn at Conder Green (just a stone's throw from Glasson) as a base and taking the canal towpath on the way down to Garstang, there's some wonderful country to explore in both directions along fairly easy and flat terrain. Like the day trip north of Glasson, this southern loop is both scenic and interesting with plenty of good hostelries and cafes en route. And it's well worth doing the overnight stop at the Stork, if only to soak up its 300 years of history and sample the pub's unbeatable full breakfast.

Glasson Dock

Midland Hotel - Morecambe

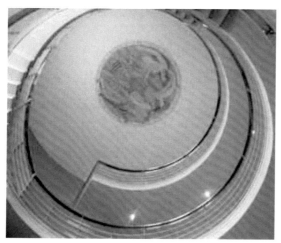

The beautiful spiral staircase at
the Midland

Morecambe Bay

Sunset over the Bay

Heysham Village

St Patrick's Church

Graveyard - Heysham

The Stork Inn at Condor Green on the Lune Estuary

Extended Tour

The one thing that's better than going cycling for the day is going cycling for a few days. Even if just for the weekend, there's a definite feeling of escape, a sense of getting away from it all and, perhaps more positively, that warm tingle of excitement at the thought of grabbing a mini holiday. As with all enjoyment, there comes responsibility, though in long-haul terms this might seem no more than a mild case of 'upping the anti'. Nevertheless, the extended bike ride does demand a definite shift in thinking.

Booking your overnight stays, packing those essentials, poring over maps and setting distances and destinations are all crucial to the success of a longer trip. You'll need as much gear for a few days as you would for a few weeks and all weather conditions have to be taken into account. Maintenance issues must also be considered - it's important to be self-sufficient. A bike shop may never be more than 20 miles away, but you've got to make sure that you carry enough spares and tools to overcome any basic problems. Due to the extra weight and mileage involved, your machine needs to be in A1 nick in any case, with panniers balanced so that it handles efficiently on the road. As with the bike, the body will have to cope with the added stress as well. Unless you're used to daily cycling, you'll wince when you get back in the saddle on the second morning. Thankfully, within a few miles, that usually disappears and wearing the right kit and having the right saddle will minimise the discomfort. Maintaining a good level of fitness and keeping yourself hydrated helps too. Like everything else in life, preparation is key.

Coast to Coast (TPT)

The Trans Pennine Trail (TPT) is a multi-user, long-distance, coast to coast journey - what a mouthful! From Southport on the Irish Sea to Hornsea on the North Sea, it incorporates the ports of Liverpool and Hull and is an integral part of the European long-distance walkers route E8. This, eventually, will go all the way from the west coast of Ireland to Istanbul! Well served by rail and bus at both ends, the TPT's 215 miles

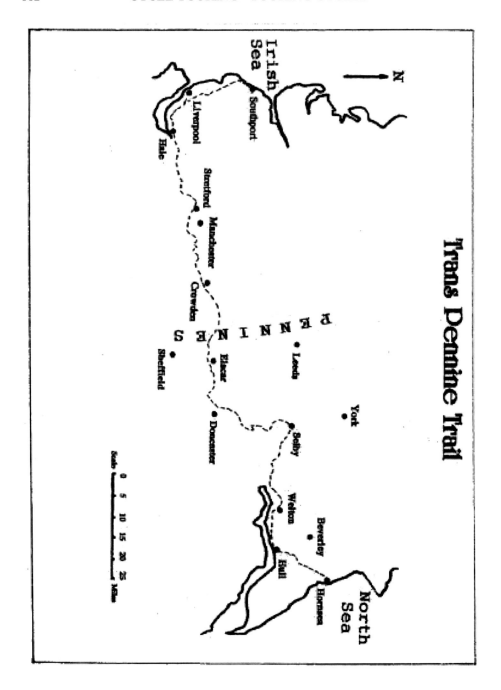

takes most cyclists 4 or 5 days to complete, depending on how many attractions and places of interest you get sidetracked by. Although you'll have to keep to some sort of schedule, remember that touring is not just about eating up the miles; do stop when you get the itch to explore your surroundings.

The trail itself is mostly easy. Apart from a steep and fairly rough section over the Pennines, much of it is, at worst, undulating and makes good use of minor roads, canal towpaths, disused railway paths, designated cycle ways and bridleways. More than 60 per cent is traffic free and the scenery you'll encounter is as varied as the surfaces you'll cycle on. It is a well thought out and a well sign-posted route.

Throughout, there is an embarrassment of accommodation available from humble campsites to hostels, welcoming guesthouses and posh hotels. Likewise with eateries; breakfast can be had at Crowden YHA in the foothills of the Pennines; you can lunch at the Old Vicarage Tea Room in Penistone or the Glove Works Riverside Mill near Glossop. You can take a break for a cream tea at Laxton village store on the way from Selby to the Humber and top up your calories with an evening meal at any one of the hundreds of pubs, cafes, restaurants and chippies en route. If nothing else, there's little chance of sleeping rough or going hungry on this trek.

We started our journey on the coastal plain just north of Liverpool (cycling west to east is best to take advantage of the prevailing wind). The time-honoured tradition of dipping your wheel in the Irish Sea is a harder job than you might think as you stare across the sands at Southport for something vaguely resembling water. And if you stare in the other direction, it's dunes and wide fields for as far as the eye can see - whoever said that the earth was flat probably came from round here!

From Southport's main promenade where a board marks the beginning of the TPT, we made our way along the front and then down between huge sand dunes at Birkdale. Heading inland via a stretch of disused rail line took us towards Aintree race course and Liverpool. Through steep cuttings and tunnels, which gave a pleasant sense of detachment from the surrounding Liverpool suburbs, Walton, Knotty Ash and then Childwall come and go. Finally, we emerged at Halewood on a purpose-built cycle path that threaded its way through a modern industrial scene and past John Lennon Airport, before getting back to cross-country tracks and semi-rural lanes. Having started late morning, our first day ended at Church End farm in the pretty village of Hale on the Mersey Estuary, but how you split each day's cycling and organise each night's stopover is very much down to choice.

Next morning, after a superb breakfast, it was bags back on the bikes and an easy cycle down to the estuary with views over Runcorn Bridge and the heavy industry on the opposite bank. More off-road riding by the canal and then a 10 miles stretch of disused rail line guided us across the Cheshire plain and brought us to the outskirts of Greater Manchester. Following the Mersey Valley on a mix of minor roads, cycle paths and riverside cycle ways led to Stockport town centre and then out again via the Tame Valley. A long day (almost 50 miles), but virtually flat all the way and with genuine points of interest and dramatic scenery at places where you might not expect them. Our accommodation for the second night was just outside the small town of Hadfield, famous for its setting as Royston-Vasey in the black comedy series 'League of Gentlemen' - well worth a stroll up the main street, where memorabilia of the show is on sale in the local shops.

The next section was, perhaps, more typical of what was to come. Open country with wide vistas dotted with villages and towns, and much of it off-road. The initial stretch from Hadfield to the Yorkshire town of Elsecar was, however, the most demanding of the whole route. Here, the TPT becomes the Longdendale Trail and climbs steadily past reservoirs and small settlements to the old railway tunnel at Woodhead. A short but extremely steep and rocky bridleway then took us over windswept moorland to the highest point of the journey at Windle Edge where, depending on the time of year, cloud can descend and temperatures drop. This was the only point where the bikes actually lost traction and we had to get off and push. The worst over, a length of newly laid tarmac freewheeled us back down to meet the trail again and then onwards to the market town of Penistone. From here, it was more open agricultural land to the next overnight stop at the Old Bank House in Elsecar.

Day four began with a quick look round the Elsecar Heritage Centre. Here I learned that the town's name had its roots in Saxon times and a local warlord called 'Elsie' - very odd. Then, a short trek back to the TPT and, after a few miles, the trail eventually took us off the western edge of the Pennines onto fairly flat countryside. Following the course of the beautiful Don Gorge with the imposing Conisbrough Castle in the distance, we were diverted along side roads to Bentley. From here, the surface becomes variable - some on-road and some fairly muddy off-road sections until you join the New Junction Canal towpath near Sykehouse. This was a pleasant part of the route, taking in delightful villages along quiet country lanes towards Snaith.

The final stretch of the TPT for this part of the journey joins the Selby Canal all the way into the market town of Selby itself, where we'd booked a room at the Willows Guesthouse - an excellent B&B and just a short walk to the centre and the town's stunning Abbey. We were now facing our last day of the trip and a final push of 54 miles.

With good weather and a following wind, we cycled east out of Selby along the banks of the River Ouse. This was possibly the prettiest section of the entire coast to coast route. Mostly along country lanes and empty minor roads, we passed through the picturesque settlements of Laxton, Ellerker and Brantringham before stopping off for lunch at Welton. Bathed in warm sunshine, we sat by the village church (which had its very own moat) and found it a bit of a struggle to get going again afterwards. Another couple of miles saw us back on the Humber Estuary and cycling beneath the spectacular Humber Bridge, one of the longest single-span suspension bridges in the world. Then into the old port of Hull with its impressive Victorian buildings, beautiful gardens and relaxed waterfront.

Threading our way through the city centre, we crossed the river and rejoined the trail heading north-east towards Hornsea. Easy riding virtually all the way along a disused rail track for 15 or so miles and then finally, as the sun began to dip, we reached the seafront. A quick photo shoot at the Coast to Coast marker, followed by a celebratory pint before finding our B&B for the night. As always, a feeling of accomplishment, relief and slight sadness that it was now over.

The Ride

Day	Destination	Bike Mileage
1	Southport - Hale	30
2	Hale - Hadfield	48
3	Hadfield - Elsecar	39
4	Elsecar - Selby	44
5	Selby - Hornsea	54

Total mileage - 215

Average daily mileage - 43

Start of the TPT at Southport · · · · · · · · · Ainsdale beach

Runcorn Bridge on the Mersey Estuary

Hadfield – better known as Royston-Vasey from the 'League of Gentlemen'

Approaching the foothills of the Pennines

Skirting the Longdendale Resevoir

Highest point of TPTat Windle Edge

Old railway tunnel near Oxpring

Heritage Centre at Elsecar

Bridge over the Don Gorge

Part of the canal section of the Trail near Selby

Selby town centre with the Abbey in the distance

Power station near Selby

Welton village church

The Humber Bridge

Hull city centre

Princes Quay waterfront - Hull

TPT signpost at Hornsea

The Expedition

The dictionary defines 'expedition' as 'an organised journey to attain some object such as exploration.' This implies a definite purpose, which is exactly what a long-distance trip should be about. Its primary purpose is, naturally, to get to where you're going and, then, get back - hopefully in one piece. But for me, the other objective of an expedition is to experience something a little different, sample a taste of adventure and, perhaps, store up some memories for your 'rocking-chair days'.

There are few opportunities in our modern, over-protected world to really put ourselves on the line, to take a risk, to follow that dream. In cycling terms, there's certainly nothing very frightening about riding round country lanes for the day and taking the occasional break for a cream-tea. Even extended bike trips, such as the 'coast to coast', hold few fears when set against a backdrop of being rarely more than a couple of miles from civilisation and having the added safety net of the mobile phone. An expedition, on the other hand, requires a slightly different mindset, in which the risk factor does have to be taken into account, but this, once more, is a matter of degree. It can be made as close to 'safe' as you want by going on an organised tour where virtually everything is done for you, or by arranging your own trip with a group of trusted friends. If travelling independently, there are still the obvious precautions you can take to stack the odds in your favour as far as risk is concerned. Much of this is done at the preparation stage and, if everything's organised well, little should go wrong - but, then again, 'the best-laid plans of mice and men ......'

It's not about being pessimistic, more about being realistic and having the right mentality to cope with any problems that might occur in the weeks you're on the road. Obviously, there can be no better feeling than returning home after the 'perfect' long-haul journey with not even a puncture to report, and that can happen. But, when things do go wrong, when a spoke snaps or you arrive in town during a festival and there's no room at the inn or the chicken you ate last night jumps back out of your throat in the morning, then you've just got to be able to deal with it.

The Baltic and Northern Europe - Helsinki to Rotterdam

It would be impossible in the space of a few short pages to fully document such a trip and, at the same time, do it justice. Instead, I hope that the following gives a flavour of the countries I travelled through and of long (but enjoyable) days in the saddle.

Few regions in the world have experienced as much change in recent years as the Baltic. Latvia, under the Soviet heel for half a century, is one of three Baltic states that now looks increasingly to the West for its economic and political future, but with a suspicious eye still fixed warily on its Russian neighbour. Russia's meddling in Georgia, where tanks lined the streets of South Ossetia to allegedly protect the migrant minority, leaves Latvia (as well as Estonia and Lithuania) feeling understandably nervous. Like the other satellite states, Latvia has a large ethnic Russian population, which the motherland continues to view as its ultimate responsibility and good enough reason for it to interfere at will. Regardless of the newly adopted ideals of democracy in the Baltic and the reassurance afforded by NATO membership, memories of the oppressive communist regime remain fresh.

   I cycled into Latvia's capital, Riga, on a pleasant afternoon and booked a room at the Backpackers Hostel. Nestled behind the city's huge Central Market, the Backpackers is a converted warehouse and rather smart for a hostel, having been upgraded to meet a growing tourist demand. After freshening up in my spacious, ensuite dorm, I wandered down to the bar for a relaxing drink only to find it absolutely heaving and with a disco in full swing. Lively Russian music pulsated in sync with rows of flashing lights and there were some real 'sorts' on the dance floor, which certainly added to the atmosphere of chaotic abandon - although all very friendly, even infectious. Plenty of noise and laughter, with many of the revellers obviously enjoying a beer or ten, judging by the number of bodies slumped in dimly lit corners and tables groaning with empty bottles. There was a real party feel about it that wouldn't have looked out of place on New Year's Eve, even though this was just another sun-washed Saturday evening in mid-August. One man I spoke to at the bar sighed

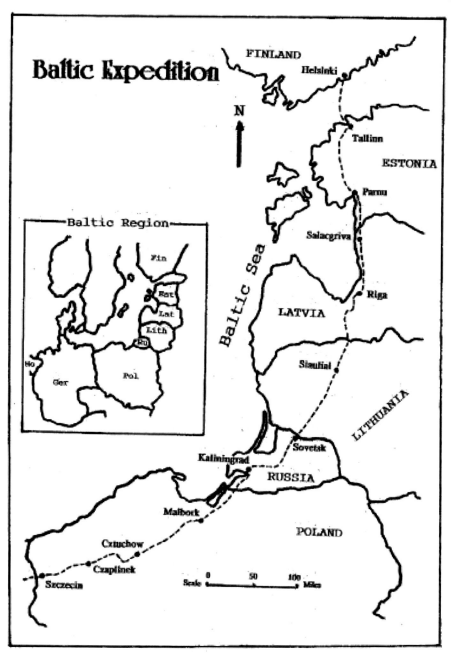

apologetically and told me that 'happiness was definitely over-rated', but with the country in recession, happiness and a few beers was about all that most people could still afford.

I'd started my journey some days earlier in Helsinki. This was for two reasons; firstly, I'd never been to Helsinki and, secondly, there was no direct flight to Tallinn, which is where I really wanted to start from. Compromise had kicked in before I'd even turned a pedal in anger, as taking a direct flight to Helsinki would be far less risky than a change of flight on my way to Tallin and the possibility of losing my luggage and bike in transit.

Having been impressed by Helsinki's riverside cycle ways and pretty waterfront, I was less impressed with the £20 'snacks' and took the early morning ferry to Estonia. Tallinn was a revelation - a stunning medieval walled town set on cobbled streets with towering fairytale spires and picturesque squares. Getting lost in its winding alleyways among the 15th century merchant houses, ancient churches and courtyards was easy, and I spent most of the day just drifting around, soaking up the atmosphere and the sights. Following the disappointment of the previous night's burger and chips al fresco, I sat down that evening to a really good home-cooked meal in a candle-lit bar near the main square, and at half the price. A couple of beers later, I was ready for bed.

After the excesses of Tallinn, some serious cycling took place. Over 80 miles initially to the west coast spa resort of Parnu, and then a 50 and a 60 mile trek into Latvia and to Riga. These first few days were bathed in warm sunshine but, being locked into a strong headwind, any advantage gained from the good weather and the flat, well-surfaced roads was lost. Carrying full packs and plodding down long, straight stretches through mile after mile of pine forest only added to the hard work of never quite being able to lose the wind. At times like this, it's good to let your mind wander. Mine was strangely focussed on the 'road kill' - lots of mink-like creatures, a black stork, a beaver and a very large cat, which certainly didn't look domestic.

Riga itself is centred on the Old Town, just a ten minute walk from the market and another Baltic gem of medieval architecture. In the

Ratslaukums (Town Hall Square) stands the ornate façade of the Blackhead's House, the home of the Guild of German bachelor merchants. This was a place famed for its wild parties (nothing new there then) and, on a snowy Christmas Eve in 1510, the boys went on a drunken rampage, returning to the square some hours later with a huge pine tree. Although their celebration of covering the tree with flowers and then setting fire to it gives a slightly different take on the ritual, the tradition of 'decorating the Christmas Tree' had been born. An octagonal plaque on the cobbled forecourt of the Blackhead's House marks the spot where the very first tree stood.

On my last morning in Latvia it rained and, for a while, progress was stop-start, taking shelter wherever I could and making up the miles as it eased. By lunchtime I'd reached the Lithuanian border and the sun magically reappeared. No Customs and no formalities - in fact, it was completely deserted apart from a small kiosk that doubled as a money exchange. At the picturesque town of Joniscos, I stopped for a well-earned meal and got chatting to a one-legged American at the next table. Now retired and residing in Kansas, he'd lived here as a child and still had relatives in a nearby village. He recounted some interesting tales about the post-war Soviet occupation and the suffering that he and his family had undergone before escaping to America. He also told me about the Hill of Crosses, a short detour on my route south. This was an incredible place, a landscape crowded with thousands of elaborately decorated crosses - some huge, some small. Made of wood and metal, these crosses commemorated lives past and were also put up by pilgrims visiting the nearby monastery. Even on a hot afternoon, busy with visitors and tourists, the hill had a strange and eerie feel about it.

A further 5 miles down the road was Siauliai (pronounced *Showlay*), where I found an excellent room at the local college for £7. Broad pedestrian avenues lined with cafes and bars, friendly people and the bonus of a bicycle museum near the centre made it another memorable overnight stop.

From Siauliai, it was a long 80 miles plus day to get to the Russian border. The weather was warm and the terrain was up and down, which made the going harder, but at least it gave some welcome shelter from the headwind. I cycled part of the way with a German couple who'd also come down from Riga. They were eventually aiming for Vilnius in central Lithuania and, after sharing lunch at a roadside café near Kelme, they headed east and I continued south. By 4 o'clock, I'd joined the long line of cars and lorries at the frontier. Beaurocracy kicked in with a vengeance - an hour to have my passport and visa checked, then forms to plough through in duplicate, bags searched and a disbelieving look when asked where I'd cycled from.

The Russian border town of Sovetsk was in complete contrast to the neat little towns of the northern Baltic. Here, broken cobbled streets were fronted by grim looking high-rises and boarded up shops - a real feel of despondency about the place. At what I assumed to be the centre, stood a large statue of Lennin, looming high in front of the 'Hotel Russia 1969', the only hotel in town. Surprisingly posh inside, this would have been a state run establishment in Soviet times and built primarily for visiting government officials. The nice lady at reception handed me another raft of paperwork to fill in (both for myself and my bike) and then showed me to my room. Breakfast, the next morning, was possibly the best I'd had so far. A huge buffet table with everything you could imagine from poached eggs to poached salmon, all set out beneath an equally huge mural of former Russian Premier, Leonid Brezhnev. No matter where you sat in the elegantly furnished room, his watchful gaze seemed to be fixed on your particular table.

Later that day and sixty-odd miles on, I arrived in Kaliningrad. Much, much bigger and spread out than I'd imagined and with atrocious roads that were badly pot-holed and carved by tramlines. This used to be the magnificent city of Konigsberg when ruled by the German kingdom of Prussia, but little survives of its original architecture other than a few medieval ruins and the cathedral. The city's castle was demolished in the 1960's to make way for the 'House of Soviets' - a grey and hideous concrete block. Although never actually used by the communist authorities, it now stands as a reminder of the ugliness of purely utilitarian structures. Like Sovetsk, Kaliningrad also appeared to have its fair share of drunks and beggars. The market economy has undoubtedly created wealth here but, at the same time, has left many floundering in its

wake and, without the security of the communist system, some seem
unable to cope.

On my ride out of Russia towards Poland, the wind suddenly dropped
and the sun came out. At Mamanova, a pleasant little town near the
border, I stopped off for a coffee and managed to exchange the last of my
Russian coins for some fruit and a packet of biscuits. A couple of miles
further on brought the checkpoint and yet another long queue, with
vehicles being searched and travellers looking hot and frustrated. I
chanced my luck and pushed my bike past the line of cars to the passport
control office and, to my amazement, the Russian border guard gave my
papers a cursory glance and waved me through. At the Polish side, my
luck ran out. I was spotted by an eagle-eyed policewoman and even
though I smiled appealingly and explained that I was English and
therefore not very bright, I was nevertheless made to empty all my bags
and then sent back to the end of the queue like a naughty schoolboy.

By now, I'd already completed well over a third of my journey, both in
terms of time and distance. Both the bike and the body were holding up
well. A slight cold and the loss of the clanger on my bell was the sum
total of my problems and I was now travelling south-west along better
roads with just a crosswind to cope with.

My first stopover in Poland was Malbork, an eighty mile cycle from
Kaliningrad. I arrived in the early evening, having twice got lost and then
forced onto a long stretch of motorway in increasingly hot weather. The
centre of Malbork, affluent looking and focussed round a monumental
fortress, was just a stone's throw from the Hotel Grot, my (anything but
grotty) home for the night. I even managed to get a new bell at a cycle
shop nearby - far better than the one I'd broken and chosen from a line of
five, which the shop assistant was only too pleased to give a
demonstration 'tinkle' on. Up and out by 8 o'clock the next day to a
strangely quiet town centre - so quiet, that I asked a passer-by whether it
was Friday or Saturday, having thought I'd maybe lost a day somewhere.
It was only when I got to my next destination, Zblewo, that I realised I
was an hour earlier than my watch showed and that I'd been running on
Russian time for the past day and a half.

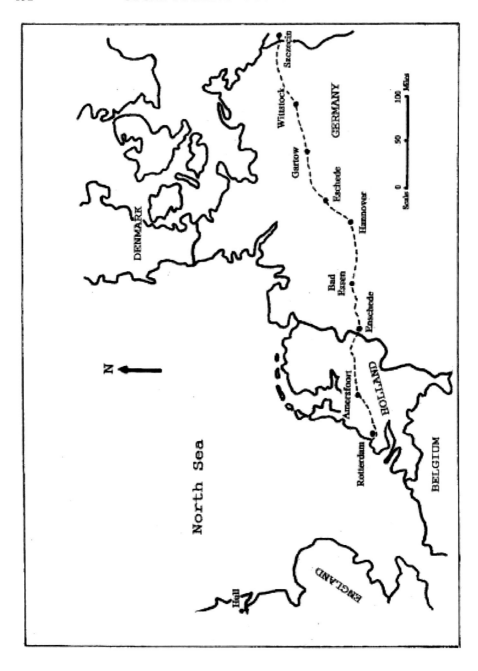

I spent almost a week cycling across Poland and was endlessly impressed by its beautiful scenery and friendly people, not to mention the wonderful weather, excellent food and cheap beer. I'd witnessed a medieval festival in the castle grounds at Cztuchow, got caught up in a wedding reception at a lakeside hotel near Czaplinek and had a game of football with a group of lads in a park in Starogard Gdansk. My final stop was at Szczecin, an unexpectedly stunning city on the border with Germany. Giving myself a rest day here, I took time out to stroll along the banks of the River Odra and roam round the centre with its beautiful parks and charming squares - a welcome break from the pattern of the past few days.

I was now pedalling my way into country number seven. Germany, like Poland, is another much ignored tourist destination and I always struggle to see just why that is. Hospitable and cycle friendly, Germany is steeped in history and enriched with fairytale castles, gingerbread architecture and romantic rivers. The accusing finger that points to it being overly organised and too well-ordered actually works to your advantage as a traveller. Accommodation is usually faultless (and far less expensive than you'd think), food is excellent and filling and German beer is, perhaps, the one thing that certainly doesn't require justification. Whatever impressions we have of Germans abroad, it's one of the few cultures I know that has a special phrase for being 'friendly to visitors' (Gast freundlich), and it shows.

The route westwards took me towards the Mecklenburg Lake District along superb cycle paths that stretched from one town to the next and cut through some wonderful countryside. I had 'elevenses' of coffee and a huge slab of plum cake at a café in Neustrelitz and lunch was a large plateful of liver, onions, mashed potato and salad in the main square at Mirow under clear blue skies. If it wasn't for the cycling, I think I could have easily developed an eating disorder in Germany.

By the time I reached Wittstock, I'd done 76 miles and was feeling hungry yet again. A beer festival had taken over the town centre and the place was buzzing, with stalls offering every manner of food and drink you could imagine. On the down side, accommodation was at a premium.

All the same, after asking round, I managed to find a 'zimmer' in a tiny terraced house nearby and a real bargain at just 17 euros for bed and breakfast. As evening turned to night, the party atmosphere showed no signs of abating. I'd arranged to meet up with a guy who was staying at the same guesthouse for a few beers. He'd been working in the area as a building subcontractor, putting in long hours for big pay and he certainly knew how to enjoy his time off. My head hit the pillow at midnight, but it was well after 2 am when I heard my friend stagger up the stairs.

As I set off the following morning, the temperature was already nudging 25 degrees and it was forecast to get even hotter. This was to be the norm for the next few days but, again, good cycle paths and plenty of places to stock up on water made the going relatively easy. At one point, I ended up on the River Elbe cycle way, tracing its meandering course for over 20 miles before heading west again towards Hannover. Beautiful old towns and villages along the way and excellent 'overnighters' in a mixture of friendly gasthoffs and small B&B's. At Hannover, I had another rest day, staying at my uncle's house north of the city and managing to squeeze in a tram ride to the centre and a raucous street-party at night. Again, copious amounts of food was washed down with good German beer and everyone seemed genuinely interested in my quest to get to Rotterdam, offering advice on the best roads to take and the places to avoid. Feeling a little the worse for wear in the morning but with a nice clean bike, I was waved off by my uncle and his neighbours who, in the cold light of day, now had that 'stupid Englander' look in their eyes.

From Hannover, I followed the route of the Mittelandkanal, spending my last night in Germany in the small town of Bad Essen. A final push of sixty miles then took me over the border and into the Dutch city of Enschede.

Holland, more correctly called the Netherlands (Holland is just the strip of land nearest the coast), is extremely flat and home to the famous 'sit up and beg' large-wheeled bicycle. These machines are seen mainly in towns and cities, effortlessly gliding through the streets and usually mounted by people in casual everyday dress. So, theoretically, the

Netherlands should be the ideal country for cyclists, but this only applies if you're heading in the right direction. The prevailing wind, which whistles relentlessly from west to east, is great if it's at your back. Unfortunately, I was going the other way and, at times, the cycling became a grim battle, only finding respite when travelling through the more built-up areas.

From Enschede, I completed the remaining 140 miles to the coast over 3 days, stopping at Apeldoorn and Gouda. Passing through Rotterdam's striking city centre, my route to Europoort took me across the Maas River. This involved taking a lift a long way underground and then continuing along a purpose-built cycle track, which passed under the river and then up a second lift to the other side - an impressive if rather spooky 'crossing'. With the estuary now on my right and the cycle path running high up on a dyke, I was completely open to the strong headwind coming off the North Sea. This final 15 mile stretch was possibly the hardest of the whole trip, having to repeatedly stand on my pedals to push my way towards the port. I arrived at the P&O terminal with just an hour to spare before the ferry set sail for Hull, feeling a mixture of relief and immense satisfaction. My Cateye read 1290 miles and I'd had no punctures, no broken spokes, absolutely nothing apart from the broken bell. In the end, even that particular cloud turned out to have a silver lining.

The Ride

Day	Destination	Bike Mileage	Accommodation	Comments
1	Manchester - Helsinki	14	hotel	flight
2	Helsinki - Tallinn	4	hostel	ferry
3	Tallinn - Parnu	81	hostel	
4	Parnu	-	hostel	rest day
5	Parnu - Salacgriva	49	school	
6	Salacgriva - Riga	63	hostel	
7	Riga	-	hostel	rest day
8	Riga - Siauliai	80	college	
9	Siauliai - Sovetsk	84	hotel	

10	Sovetsk - Kaliningrad	62	guesthouse	
11	Kaliningrad	-	guesthouse	rest day
12	Kaliningrad - Malbork	86	hotel	
13	Malbork - Zblewo	36	guesthouse	
14	Zblewo - Cztuchow	46	hotel	
15	Cztuchow - Czaplinek	62	inn	
16	Czaplinek - Szczecin	85	hostel	
17	Szczecin	-	hostel	rest day
18	Szczecin - Wittstock	80	B&B	
19	Wittstock - Gartow	71	gasthoff	
20	Gartow - Eschede	70	B&B	
21	Eschede - Hannover	38	free B&B	(uncle's)
22	Hannover - Bad Essen	74	gasthoff	
23	Bad Essen - Enschede	66	inn	
24	Enschede - Apeldoorn	45	hostel	
25	Apeldoorn - Gouda	54	hotel	
26	Gouda - Europoort	40	ferry	

Total mileage - 1290

Average daily mileage - 49.6

Estonia - Tallinn's Raekoja Plats (Town Hall Square)

St Olaf's Church - Tallinn

Strange artwork on Salacgriva's
waterfront - Latvia

Blackhead's House in Riga's Ratslaukums Square

Riga's busy tourist scene

Inside the Museum of
Occupation - Riga

Lithuania - Hill of Crosses

College B&B in Siauliai

Bicycle Museum - Siauliai

Hotel Russia 1969 - Sovetsk

Russian military memorabilia

Kaliningrad - The grim 'Dom Sovetov' (House of Soviets)

Kaliningrad's waterfront and Gothic Cathedral

'Walking dogs and driving cars forbidden'
    - not quite how I read it

The tragic side of the post-communist era

Malbork's iconic Tower - Poland

Grot Hotel in Malbork

Pomerania region of Poland

Fully 'loaded' bike

Waterfront at Szczecin on the Polish/German border

Crossing the River Elbe
in Germany

Futuristic statue on the road to Wittstock

Luchow's Ratskeller (Town Hall)

Hannover

Rotterdam's looming sky scrapers - The Netherlands

Glossary

ATB
All Terrain Bikes (sometimes called MTB) are commonly known as mountain bikes and come in many different guises (see Mountain Bike).

Bottom bracket
The bike's drive unit - the cartridge mounted axle that passes through the base of the frame.

Butterfly bars
'Figure of 8' handlebars often fitted to touring bikes to give variable hand positions over long distances.

Cadence
The rate at which you pedal - the number of revolutions of the crank per minute.

Cantilever V-brakes
A design of brake giving efficient stopping power and used on many hybrids and tourers.

Chain breaker
Tool used to 'split' a chain by pushing the pin out of the link.

Chainset
Sometimes referred to as 'chainrings', this is the group of front cogs (usually two or three) fitted to the derailleur gear system.

City bike
A bike for urban cycling - a hybrid with narrow 700c tyres, comfort saddle, bike rack, mudguards and lighting system.

Clipless pedals
Pedals that interlock with the cleats of special cycling shoes, enabling the pedals to be pulled up as well as pushed down.

Crank
The arms joining the pedals and chainset.

Derailleur gear system
A system of multiple cogs on front chainset and rear freewheel linked by a moveable chain mechanism. Usually consists of 2 or 3 cog chainset and 8, 9 or 10 cog freewheel cassette.

Disc brakes
These are brakes operated by either cable or hydraulics and involve a calliper and disc mounted on the wheel hub. Most often fitted to mountain bikes and some hybrids.

D lock
D locks (or U locks) are solid shackle-type locks made of hardened steel bar that give a high level of security.

Drivetrain
Incorporating the front chainset, rear freewheel cassette, derailleurs, bottom bracket and chain, this is the complete mechanism for driving the bike. In a hub gear system, it embodies the rear wheel hub (4 - 8 cogs), bottom bracket, front sprocket and chain.

Drop bars
Drop-style handlebars are found on all road bikes (racers) and many touring cycles. Like butterfly bars, they allow for a variety of hand positions.

Dynamo lighting system
Bottle dynamos are driven by the rotating wheel of the dynamo resting on the tyre, whereas hub dynamos are built into the wheel hub.